Suicide

in Ireland

Fergal Bowers

Publication sponsored by the Irish Medical Organisation

Published and sponsored by the
Irish Medical Organisation
10 Fitzwilliam Place
Dublin 2
Tel. 6767273

First published in 1994.

ISBN 0 9523033 0 2

The views expressed in this book are personal ones and
should not be taken as in any way representing the views of
the IMO.

Distributed by Eason & Son, Dublin, Ltd

Cover design by Denis Buckley

Printed by Colour Books Ltd,
Baldoyle, Dublin 13

ABOUT THE AUTHOR

Fergal Bowers was born in Dublin in 1961. For the last fourteen years he has worked in Ireland as a journalist. As one of Ireland's leading health correspondents, he is a regular contributor of news and analysis to both the national press and radio.

His first book, *The Work* - an examination of Opus Dei in Ireland - was published in 1989 and reached the Irish bestsellers' list.

He has wide experience in general news, investigative journalism and currently works as Senior Reporter with the prominent weekly newspaper, *Irish Medical News*. Fergal Bowers is married and lives in Dublin.

DEDICATION

For Annie Claire Bowers 1921-1990
and
Michael J Bowers 1913-1983

For all of my family and friends

CONTENTS

FOREWORD

Suicide has become a major public health issue in Ireland. Officially, over 1,000 people have taken their lives by suicide in this country in the last three years. However, the real number is known to be much greater. If as many people were killed in a plane crash or a major disaster, it would be viewed as a national tragedy. Yet, there can be little argument that each death by suicide is a tragedy, a sad commentary on modern society. The guilt and hardship a suicide imposes on the families and friends of the deceased are immeasurable. The most common reaction among relatives is surprise and shock - most people say they had no idea how desperate the suicide victim was.

In 1992, there were 354 official deaths by suicide in Ireland - the highest number ever recorded in a single year. The number of suicides continues to increase each year, in particular among young men. This book marks an attempt to look behind the grim statistics and examine how we, as a supposedly caring society, can begin to prevent this continuing, unnecessary loss of life.

Official Irish suicide figures under-record the problem, but to what degree is a matter of heated debate. Some experts claim that suicide figures of between 700-1,400 a year would more accurately reflect the picture - significantly more than the numbers killed annually in road traffic accidents. In any event, the official suicide figures must be seen as purely a baseline. Even if we are consistently underestimating the number of suicides, it is still possible to pick up increasing or decreasing trends.

The increase in suicide has been particularly marked among young men, and those in rural areas. Some believe this may be due to changes in the role of men in society and an ability among women to cope better with crises. The largest number of suicides in Ireland are among those aged between 24 and 34 years. The results of a report by Irish child psychiatrists on suicide among the under 12s - outlined in this book - also make for startling reading.

The issue of suicide gained greater prominence here during the 1992 abortion controversy. The Irish Supreme Court ruled, in the case of a 14 year-old alleged rape victim, that if there was a real and substantial risk to her life - in this case suicide - then a termination of pregnancy was permissible.

Arising from the 'X' case, a referendum aiming, among other things, to exclude threatened suicide as grounds for termination of pregnancy was rejected by the Irish people by a majority of two to one in November 1992. The wording put forward by the Fianna Fail/Progressive Democrat Government at the time specifically excluded the threat of suicide as grounds for an abortion as it was felt that this might be abused by women and would effectively open the floodgates to abortion in Ireland. The debate on the issue of suicide and abortion continues and has yet to be resolved.

An estimated 8,000-9,000 people also attempt suicide here each year, but as no official recording procedures exist to examine these cases in more detail, we can only guess at the extent of this problem. A Dublin casualty consultant estimates that around four people a day are seen at accident & emergency departments in the capital, following suicide attempts. Also, the number of non-fatal deliberate overdoses in north Dublin's inner city alone has almost trebled since 1973 and, disturbingly, many women in particular are using paracetamol on its own or with other drugs.

While the reporting of suicide has improved, only now can it be registered officially as a cause of death. Irish coroners were forbidden in law to do so until the crime of suicide was abolished in 1993.

However, the social and moral stigma of suicide remains. In the eyes of the Catholic Church, suicide in certain circumstances is still a mortal sin. The social stigma hinders research and also makes people unwilling to discuss suicide. Some leading Irish medical researchers investigating suicide in Ireland for academic purposes claim to have, in some cases, been denied access to coroner's records.

In this book there are calls for the setting up of new suicide reporting procedures. One of these new procedures would allow coroners to return confidential reports to the Central Statistics Office, to complement the existing Garda forms sent to the CSO. Such a change would certainly lead to more accurate figures being gathered and a better understanding of the extent of the problem.

In this book, prominent Cork consultant psychiatrist Dr Michael Kelleher recommends that paracetamol should not be freely available without prescription and, if it is, it should only be sold in quantities which, if taken together, would not be fatal. He also says that poisoning with car exhaust fumes could be reduced if catalytic converters were installed in all motor cars. He proposes that a expert committee be set up to produce a short but informed annual report on the trends in suicidal behaviour in this country.

Whatever the reasons for a suicide, the stigma it places on a family is as real today as it ever was. The sadness and often shame a suicide brings to a family is a life-long burden which society is duty-bound to help lift. More support for affected families is certainly needed. We can learn from the experience elsewhere. Ireland is not alone in the problem. Suicide is among the leading causes of death in a number of countries.

What causes an individual to make the biggest moral decision possible and take their own life? What are the factors which drive people to such depths of despair? It is clear that many factors influence a suicide decision, among these depression, unemployment, life crises, inability to cope, loneliness, alcohol abuse, mental illness and other social factors.

In this book, well-known Dublin consultant psychiatrist Professor Patricia Casey points out that studies now indicate, that psychiatric illness may be forming a far less important part in causing suicide and the increase may be associated with changes occurring in European society. She says that the most important message for society is that suicide is now largely a socio-political problem, rather than a medical one. As a result, the interventions must focus on changing those aspects of society which cause the conditions associated with suicide.

We know that suicide can be prevented - but to what degree? Why is it that so many people are judging life in Ireland as not worth living? One death by suicide is one too many. It is difficult to compare our official suicide rate with other countries, where suicide has not been a crime for many years; reporting procedures are different and where religious and social views may have less influence.

Quite apart from the human tragedy of suicide and attempted suicide, the cost to the health service in treating these people is enormous - millions of pounds each year.

The number of suicides in Ireland demands that the issue receives more widespread investigation by the Government as well as recognition and greater understanding by society. A national programme of suicide prevention would be welcome. In Britain, the Government has set specific targets for reducing suicides by the year 2,000.

This book, aimed at the general public, is a contribution to the long-awaited debate on suicide in Ireland. It is encouraging to note that valuable research has been undertaken and continues into suicide in Ireland by professionals from a wide range of areas.

There are many people I would like to thank for their assistance in producing this book, in particular, the Irish Medical Organisation for its foresight in recognising the value of sponsoring a 'public interest' book. Thanks also to Dr Cormac Macnamara and IMO Chief Executive, George McNeice for their help. It should be noted that the views expressed in this book must not be taken as representing the official views of the IMO. I owe a special thanks also to Senator Dan Neville, the political leader of the campaign to decriminalise suicide, for his assistance; fellow-author and multi-award winner, Paddy Doyle, for his help and encouragement; and to the many doctors, social workers and front line professionals who provided me with valuable insights, in particular, consultant psychiatrists, Dr Michael Kelleher, Professor Patricia Casey and Professor Tom Fahy.

I must also thank Niall Hunter, editor of the *Irish Medical News* and my other work colleagues for their assistance and support. Thanks also to my employers MAC Publishing, and Una O' Hare for the use of the office computer. Denis Buckley, production editor of the *Medical News* designed the cover, and assisted greatly in the final production of the book. Thanks are also due to Dr Alan Lopez, World Health Organisation, Geneva; Joyce Andrews and Sean Phillips of University College Dublin for the use of the University Library and last, but not least, my wife, Rosina, for her love and support. A special thanks is also due also to those who granted me personal interviews and the people who supplied valuable information during my three years of research.

I must record a particular note of appreciation to all those who responded to a national newspaper notice in early 1994, seeking information from people who had experiences of suicide and attempted suicide among family members and friends. Permission was sought from those whose stories are recounted, prior to publication. For reasons of privacy, certain names and places have been changed.

For those who have taken their lives - for whatever reasons - this book is a reminder that they must not be forgotten. To those who have lost loved ones through suicide, I hope this book offers some comfort through a better understanding of the problem. Finally, those wishing to contact the author are welcome to do so through the publishers.

From the outset, it must be stated that the author is not suggesting or implying that any of the persons named in this book have committed or attempted suicide, unless this is specifically stated.

CHAPTER ONE

THE SILENT DEBATE

"I assume now that death, when it finally comes, will probably be nastier than suicide and, certainly a lot less convenient."

Alfred Alvarez, The Savage God, 1971

Many of us have contemplated suicide at one time or another. However, for most people, it remains just a fleeting thought without real intent or seriousness - a short-lived reaction to depression or a life crisis. Yet, we hear of friends and others who have taken their lives and wonder what can have brought them to carry out such a final act. Can circumstances have been so bad that life was no longer worth living or, were they overcome by mental illness ? Suicide leaves so many questions unanswered. It also causes intense guilt and remorse among the family and friends of the deceased. Relatives and friends may blame themselves for missing signs of suicidal behaviour or for being unreceptive to signals of desperation. The funerals of those who have committed suicide are very different to most funerals. There is a great silence and normally talkative neighbours and friends appear tongue-tied. House-private will usually be included in the death notice and the family will feel a sense of intense isolation. Well-meaning friends may make apparently hurtful comments in an awkward attempt to console. A suicide causes tremendous isolation within a family and also, between the family and society. Family members may feel responsible; friends afraid to broach the subject and so they stay away. The opportunity to understand and live with the suicide may be lost. A caring society must learn to put aside its natural fears about suicide and talk more openly about the problem.

1

SUICIDE IN IRELAND

Where there is a suspicion that a family member may be thinking about suicide, it is important that other members of the family be open about it. Those at risk need a confidant and professional help. There are many support groups around the country for those who feel depressed and for families bereaved by a suicide. It is also important to remember that suicides tend to run in families, emphasising the need for counselling and support.

Suicide is one of the few remaining taboo subjects in Ireland. It has remained largely outside the realm of public debate - hidden as darkly as the act itself. Yet suicide leaves no-one untouched, as members of the human race we are all affected.

The impact of a death on a family is always great. Where suicide is the cause or the suspected cause, the trauma is even greater. Death is inevitable and ideally it should arrive following a long and fruitful life. Where it occurs naturally in the company of family and friends, there is much comfort. Grieving is a normal part of the bereavement process, however following a suicide, it can be powered by deep anger, resentment and guilt. Some people never recover from the shock of a suicide. There is one important principle when dealing with those bereaved by suicide, we must never make the pain worse. Suicide is a delicate subject and we must always bear in mind the grief, trauma and sorrow that families, relatives and friends have to carry following a suicide.

Around 350 people die through suicide each year here, official Government figures show. However, this is the tip of the iceberg. Some research suggests that the official figure could be multiplied by a factor of between 2-4 to gain a true figure. Most of us are aware of people who it is believed committed suicide. In cases where there are signs that a drowning has occurred, the body may never be recovered. The absence of a body to mourn adds to the family anguish and uncertainty.

It is estimated that more people die through suicide in Ireland than are killed on our roads each year. Depression is one of the key causes, but it is not the only cause. There can be a host of contributing factors to a suicide. Suicides appear to peak in

Spring and early summer.

In 1992, there were 354 'official' suicides in Ireland - the highest number ever recorded in a single year. When the figures come available for 1993, they are expected to be similar. Around three quarters of all suicides are among men, one quarter among women. A small number of suicides are recorded each year among children.

The number of suicides has been increasing in recent years. A small part of the increase in official suicide figures may be due to a wider acceptance of suicide as a cause of death and less reticence by the authorities to register deaths as such. However, the moral and social stigma attached to the act of suicide must always be taken into account when we examine the official figures. Until very recently, suicide was also a crime. For understandable reasons, suicides have remained a hidden factor in Irish society. There is the legendary case of an Irish coroner who in 1967, returned a verdict of accidental death on a man who had shot himself. The incident was reported by Mary Holland in *The Observer* newspaper at the time. It was the coroner's verdict that the deceased had been "cleaning the muzzle of the gun with his tongue."

Around 200,000 Irish people have a depressive illness. Depression costs the country over £250 million a year, with much of this cost carried by the loss to business due to sick leave. People may not realise that the cause of their feeling anxious, tired or being unable to sleep, is due to depression. There also remains a stigma attached to depression which results in some of those affected failing to seek help or admit they are suffering from the condition. In recent years, the Samaritans Organisation in Ireland has been dealing with an increasing number of calls from depressed and suicidal people, some of a very young age. For many people, the Samaritans is the last resort, the end of the line. What the Samaritans operate is a listening and befriending service, they never advise or judge callers. The Dublin branch is the busiest after London and handles over 74,000 calls a year. The branch has six emergency lines and often, such is the demand, that all of the lines are engaged. Around one in every hundred callers have attempted suicide at the time of the call. An even greater number are actively thinking of suicide at the time. Many of the callers are elderly people, particularly prone to isolation, depression and feelings of despair. The work of the Samaritans is to be greatly admired. The befriending service is always available, through the help of volunteers, at any hour of the day or night for those passing through personal crisis. Although their aim of preventing suicide is not reflected in a reduction in suicide rates, the number of suicides they help prevent is an unknown quantity. This issue was raised at the annual conference of the Institute of Guidance Counsellors in Galway in early 1994. A child psychiatrist, Dr Tony O' Carroll, quoting British research, said there was no evidence that counselling agencies such as the Samaritans reduced the suicide rate. The professional and medical services seemed to have done better, he added. It seems likely that while the Samaritans generally reach the attempted suicide group, they have little effect on the psychotic suicide who is unlikely to contact them. Despite this, the vital lifeline that the Samaritans offer the lonely and suicidal must be cherished and developed. Another organisation which receives little publicity is AWARE, the voluntary group founded in 1985 to help those with depression and recurrent mood disorders. The organisation, spearheaded by Dr Patrick McKeon of St. Patrick's Hospital, operates a special 'depression phone line' in Dublin. It is the only specific phoneline counselling service in Europe for people with depression. AWARE centres receive around 6,000 calls a year.

"Around half of all calls are from family and friends, worried about someone who is depressed. We work closely with the Samaritans," Dr McKeon says. AWARE is also part-funding a major research project into the genetics of depression and manic depression at Trinity College Dublin. It has provided over £120,000 for the multi-centre project in the last four years. Two Irish researchers are examining depression within 10 Irish fami-

4

lies as part of the project.

It is important however, that the Irish Government's responsibility to ensure that the social services are equipped to deal with the twin problems of suicide and attempted suicide does not rest disproportionately on the shoulders hard-working voluntary groups. In the aftermath of a suicide it can be easy to forget that the families affected require long-term counselling.

One organisation which has done marvellous work is the Friends of the Suicidally Bereaved in Cork, set up by two housewives, Lynn Homan and Theresa Millea.

"After a suicide the hardest things to cope with are the sense of lonliness, the violence of the act, especially if it happens in a person who was very gentle, and until recently the criminal tag," says Theresa.

Underreporting of suicide is accepted to be widespread in many countries, including Ireland. The extent of the concealment depends on the way we record and certify deaths, as well as the influence of local taboos. Until recently, suicide was a common law offence here. It was not created by Statute but formed part of the ancient unwritten law of England, as interpreted by judges. Why it was made an offence is unclear, but the reason is probably because suicide was regarded as self-murder. In Ireland, deaths which should have been recorded as suicide have been classified as open verdicts or as 'accidental drowning', 'accidental poisoning' or 'injury undetermined whether accidental or purposely self-inflicted'. If deaths are now being more correctly classified as suicide then we should see a decrease in the number recorded as 'accidental'. This has not happened to any noticeable extent in Ireland, which suggests that the increase is very real. Back in 1966, the official suicide figures in Ireland came in for scrutiny by two doctors. They obtained permission from the Dublin City and County Coroners to examine records for the years 1954-63, irrespective of the verdicts returned. Their investigation revealed that the true rate was seriously underreported in the Central Statistics Office figures. However, it was conceded that suicide rates here were low at the time, in comparison with other countries. A more recent Irish study has shown that there is likely to have been a two fold increase in real suicide during the past twenty years.

Establishing some years later, on the basis of coroner's records, whether a death was suicide or not, poses major problems for investigators. Doctors and Gardai at the time of the death may have been in the possession of vital information surrounding the incident, unavailable to investigators in later years. An example would be a death in the family or a row.

In any event, when researchers have tried to unravel the true picture of suicide in Ireland, some have been hampered by the authorities. Even doctors working for the State-funded Health Research Board have faced this obstacle:

"We were denied direct access to coroners' records in Dublin but were supplied with those cases thought to be suicide by the coroners," Do statistics lie? (Dr Dermot Walsh and others, 1990)

The Central Statistics Office classify deaths as suicide from information supplied by the investigating Garda on a special form supplied for the purpose. This is known as Form 104. The form is sent along with the coroner's death certificate to the CSO in Dublin. Where there is any suspicion of foul play, the Gardai contact the coroner and the state pathologist. Irish coroners were effectively barred from recording an official verdict of suicide at inquests after 1985 when, for the first time, a coroner's verdict of suicide was appealed to the High Court. According to the Coroners Act of 1962, Sections 30 and 31:

"Questions of civil or criminal liability shall not be considered or investigated at an inquest and accordingly every inquest shall be confined to ascertaining the identity of the person in relation to whose death the inquest is being held and how, when and where the death occurred. Neither the verdict nor any rider to the verdict at an inquest shall contain a censure or exoneration of any person."

This effectively meant that at inquests, coroners were only permitted to make recommendations of a general nature designed to prevent further fatalities. Suicide cannot be presumed. Unlike the pathologist who examines the body, a coroner only investigates the circumstances surrounding the death, having been provided with the pathologist's report. At its most basic, the purpose of the coroner's inquest is to answer four key questions: who the deceased was, when and where he or she died and how the death occurred. Inquests however examine the circumstances in great detail and many witnesses may be called to give evidence. Inquests are open to the public and the evidence given is done so under oath. Each year, coroners are obliged to make returns to the Minister for Justice on the inquests held in their district. The way in which coroners practice can vary from one district to another and coroners have a certain amount of discretion in their role.

Until 1993, under Irish law, suicide was a felony and attempted suicide, a misdemeanour. A person convicted of attempting suicide was liable to a fine or imprisonment or both. While imposing a penalty on someone who committed suicide did not arise, the family suffered greatly. It is nothing short of astonishing that in modern Ireland, many very depressed people whose mental balance may have been impaired should, following suicide, have had a criminal offence attached to their final act of desperation. If it was intended to act as a deterrent, then it failed miserably. In effect it penalised the family, innocent people already hit by the tragedy of the event. Not until the Criminal Law (Suicide) Act, became law in 1993 were the offences of suicide and attempted suicide finally abolished. A new offence of aiding or abetting suicide was introduced with a maximum penalty of up to 14 years for those convicted under this section. The battle to have the law changed was spearheaded by Senator Dan Neville from Limerick. The history of his campaign is dealt with in a later chapter. It had its beginnings in a young Fine Gael motion passed by the Tralee branch of the party in November 1990, attended by Senator Neville. He later introduced a private members Bill in the Senate in 1991 to decriminalise suicide. However, it was voted down by the then Minister for Justice, Mr Ray Burke who pledged to bring in a similar measure. Senator Neville persisted in his campaign, backed by a number of coroners and doctors who argued strongly that those who attempted suicide required compassion and care and not the attention of the criminal law. To hold a person criminally liable for killing themselves is clearly wrong. Even in a murder trial, allowance is made for diminished responsibility. It can be fairly said that most people who take their own lives are not in a normal frame of mind at the time. However, it was not until 1993 that the reform of the old suicide law was finally promised, as part of the new Fianna Fail/Labour programme for government. With the change in legislation, it has been argued that coroner's courts should in future be held in private, like the family law courts. It has also been suggested that coroners write confidential reports on all suicide cases before them and that these reports be sent to the Central Statistics Office. Such a move would allow the authorities to see what the trends in suicide are in different parts of the country and possibly help intervention planning. How does Dan Neville now view the future, given that his campaign has been a success.

"We must continue to remove the stigma and taboo connected with suicide. It has only partially been removed with the change in the law. I certainly hope that people now see suicide as a social rather than a criminal problem. We must now concentrate our efforts to develop a better understanding of why there is an increase in suicide, especially among young people. Suitable suicide prevention programmes should be introduced for Irish society. In America these programmes are already in place. However, our culture is different to the Americans, so we need tailor our programmes to our society," he says.

Generally speaking, there remains a presumption against suicide in favour of an accident. The decision by the Irish High Court in April 1985 in the *State vs Scully* case, mentioned previous, seriously affected the gathering of accurate suicide figures. The court case followed the death of a man who had been struck by a train near his home in May 1984. While the inquest verdict was suicide, the wife of the deceased appealed on several grounds against the verdict to the High Court. She claimed that important evidence in her possession about the case had not been heard because no statement had been taken from her by the investigating Garda. She also claimed that she was not told of the date and place of the inquest. The evidence she had was that earlier in the morning on which her husband was found dead, he had been in high spirits and showed no signs of depression. The judge upheld the appeal because, in addition to her evidence, he said:

"It was obviously intended by Section 30 of the Act of 1962 (legislation regarding the jurisdiction of coroners) that it should not be open to a coroner's jury to bring in a verdict that a named person had unlawfully killed the deceased and, by analogy, I would hold that it was not intended that it should be open to them to find that the deceased had unlawfully brought about his own death by suicide ... it appears to me that in bringing in a finding of suicide against the deceased, the jury were considering and investigating questions both of civil and criminal liability and were going outside the functions conferred on them by the Coroners Act, 1962."

In a recent case, a Donegal woman won a High Court action to see two letters left by her brother, shortly before he drowned. The deceased and his six week old son died when their car went off a pier at Rathmullan in December, 1992. Earlier the coroner in the case had decided that he would not allow the letters be admitted into evidence. The deceased man's sister said she had never seen the letters and claimed that she had been refused sight of them. She was unable to take legal advice in relation to their contents. She challenged the case in the High Court and won the right of access to the letters.

Inquests are held by coroners when a death has occurred in a violent or unnatural manner; suddenly and from unknown causes or in suspicious circumstances. A post mortem is usually carried out.

Coroners are not allowed to inquire into the mental capacity of a person during an inquest. This follows a judgment by Mr Justice Richard Johnston in a judicial review in 1989 in the case of Green v McLaughlin. In his judgment, Mr Johnston said that the coroner was not permitted to ask about the mental capacity of the deceased "even in order to produce an innocent explanation for the actions of a self-killer". (Judicial Review No 87 of 1989.)

After the *State v Scully* judgment, coroners continued to include in their inquest verdicts, terms which implied intent like 'self-administered' or 'self-induced' but the word suicide was no longer used.

Even when it was possible to record suicide as a cause of death before the 1985 High Court case, there was a reluctance to do so. Up to 1985, a verdict of suicide was justified in law only if the evidence showed beyond all reasonable doubt that the deceased was responsible for the act which lead to his death and that he intended the act should have that outcome.

Even with the recent decriminalisation of suicide, coroners will still have to prove intent before returning a suicide verdict. While a suicide might be indicated by the medical evidence, the legal test must also be met. There will be no compulsion to return a verdict of suicide. The legal presumption against suicide will remain and is well-described in this quotation from a judge in an English case.

"Suicide must never be presumed. If a person dies a violent death, the possibility of suicide may be there for all to see, but must not be presumed merely because it seems on the face of it to be a likely explanation. Suicide must be proved by evidence, it is the duty of the coroner not to find suicide, but to find an open verdict....There are many, many cases where there is real doubt as to the cause of death and where an open verdict is right, and where anything else is unjust to the family of the deceased."

It will always be open to the family of the deceased to challenge a suicide verdict in the courts. As a result, many coroners believe that 'open verdicts' will continue to be a feature of the Irish system resulting in suicides continuing to be hidden. The change in the law however means that from now on, where the evidence indicates it, a coroner can return a verdict of suicide. But ultimately, it is up to the coroner to decide what word or phrase will be recorded to describe the cause of death. Many suicides have traditionally masqueraded as accidental drownings and these pose a major problem for investigators. Today however, the CSO is recording an increasing number of 'drownings' as suicide, where the evidence suggests so. Rivers in particular appear to be a focus point for the suicidal. The River Shannon has seen a large number of suicides, in particular on the main bridge in Athlone. There have even been calls for telephone boxes to be placed along its banks, so that those at risk can ring for help. Train lines are also the focus point of suicides and many have occurred along the DART line in Dublin.

An opportunity was missed by the Government during the law change to decriminalise suicde in 1993. In the case of the Coroner's Court, discretion should have been given to the coroner to hold inquests into cases of suspected suicide, in private. This would spare the family affected the added trauma of having the personal details of the death aired to a public gallery. Only those having business with the inquest should be present in these particular cases. Also, the whole manner in which investigations into possible suicides and inquests into these cases are held needs to be changed. The very nature of the Coroner's Court, with its jury, Garda and medical wittnesses, feeds the guilt and fear felt by each member of the family affected. The Gardai have to summon wittnesses to the court, some of these may be family members. Coroner's do their best to put witnesses and family members at ease, but more must be done. Current proceedings tend to have an air of criminality, despite the change in the law.

Because only recently legislative changes make it possible to record suicide as the official cause of death, Irish insurance companies have been faced with a real dilemma for many years. Most life assurance policies contain an exclusion clause which means that should the holder commit suicide during the first or second year of the policy, it will be deemed null and void. According to the Irish Insurance Federation, most policies have exclusion clauses of up to two years. Given however, that official death certificates could not have suicide listed as the cause of death until recently, insurance companies were not really in a position to refuse to pay out, even following a suspected suicide. Companies who refused could have found themselves in court having to prove that the death was self-inflicted; not a pleasant prospect. There are no recorded instances in Ireland where a family has yet challenged a refusal to pay out on a life policy when suicide was strongly suspected. On the other hand, few insurance companies would be anxious to fight such sensitive cases in open court, under the full glare of publicity. The IIF says that it would be very unhappy if any family were to hold off seeking payment on a policy in the fear that because their loved one may have committed suicide, the policy would not be honoured. However, with the decriminalisation of suicide, it is probably only a matter of time before such a case ends up in court. In April 1994, it was alleged that the widow of a suicide victim who had been insured with a company for many years had been subjected to a special investigation. It was claimed that the investigator had visited local pubs to gather information on the case. Some policies taken out over 20 or 30 years ago exclude payment, in the case of a suicide. Following the controversy here, the Minister for Commerce and Technology called for a more humane approach as regards insuring people who subsequently commit suicide. Minister Seamus Brennan has proposed to the Irish Insurance Federation that all life policies include a two year extension clause.

Establishing the extent of suicide in Ireland is also hampered by the fact that the Catholic Church views suicide as a mortal sin, in certain circumstances. In the past, those who killed themselves were often refused a christian burial on consecrated ground. In The Field, by Irish playwright, John B. Keane, the central character Bull McCabe is tortured throughout his life by his son's suicide. The church had refused the body to be buried on consecrated ground. Because of the final nature of the act, those who committed suicide were not even in a position to repent for their 'sin'. The Catholic Church views suicide as an interference with the prerogative of God.

According to the new universal Catechism of the Catholic Church, we should not despair of the eternal salvation of people who have killed themselves. The English version of the new Catechism is due to be issued in Ireland in late 1994. However, a translation from the French edition, already published, and provided by the Irish Catholic Press and Information Office says of suicide:

"Everyone is responsible for his or her life before the God who gave it and remains its sovereign master. We are obliged to accept life gratefully and preserve it for God's honour and our souls' salvation. We are stewards, not owners, of the life God has entrusted to us; it is not ours to dispose of.

Suicide contradicts the natural human inclination to preserve and perpetuate life. It seriously contradicts authentic self-love and love of neighbour as well because it unjustly sunders the bonds of solidarity with the family, the civic community and human society towards which we continue to have obligations. Finally, suicide is contrary to love for the living God.

If suicide is committed with the intention of giving example, especially to the young, it takes on the gravity of scandal. Voluntary co-operation in the suicide of another person is contrary to the moral law.

Serious psychological difficulties, anguish or fear of grave hardship, suffering or torture can diminish the responsibility of the person who has committed suicide.

We should not despair of the eternal salvation of persons who have killed themselves. By ways known to him alone, God can provide the opportunity for saving repentance. The Church prays for people who have taken their own lives."

How the Catholic Church and its priests deal with suicide is covered in more detail in a later chapter.

However, it is clear that times have changed and the harsh religious views have eased. Yet the stigma of the act still remains. A suicide gives everyone - including the victim, the family, friends and even clergy, an incentive to make a suicide appear to have been an accident or perhaps even a murder.

What exactly is suicide? It is the intentional and voluntary taking of one's own life. The word comes from the latin, sui, of one's self and cadre, to slay. Actually, suicide is neither a disease nor technically a cause of death. The death is caused by some-thing else - a rope, poison, a gun or some other implement. Some forms are direct such as hanging, others are indirect such as refusing to take actions necessary for self-preservation. It could be argued that hunger strikes, for example, or a refusal to allow a life-saving blood transfusion are both forms of suicide. If a person dies as a result of a self-imposed hunger strike, has he or she not failed to take actions necessary for self-preservation? The term 'partial suicide' has been used for self-mutilation and 'chronic sui-cide' for habitual behaviour patterns injurious to life. In Ireland, suicides are classified variously as: by self-inflicted poisons; by solid or liquid substances; gas in domestic use; other gases or vapours; self-inflicted injury by hanging, strangulation and suffo-cation; drowning; using firearms or explosives, cutting or piercing instruments; jumping from a high place or by other unspecified means. The method used often depends on national trends and availability of means. The commonest methods of suicide in Ireland are hanging and drowning for men and poisoning and drowning for women. The popular image of slashing one's wrists to commit suicide is actually rare in the Western World. While it is seldom successful, it is usually very painful. The blood vessels are deep in the wrist but are not generally large enough to cause lethal bleeding. Usually all the person succeeds in doing is causing a deformity in their hand by damaging nerves and muscle tendons. While overdosing on drugs is a common method, doctors have found that the horrible experience of having one's stomach literally 'pumped out' in a casualty ward is enough to stop some people from ever attempting suicide again.

Investigators have also discovered that some indirect suicides take the form of homicide-suicide, in which an individual arranges to be killed by someone else, usually because the person cannot do it or feels that it would be more moral if someone else carried out the act.

One of the major news events of 1977 in America was the attempt by convicted murderer, Garry Gilmore, to have the State of Utah execute him. Gilmore tried to kill himself when it appeared that the state might not, but his own attempt failed. In the end, the state executed him by firing squad. He was the first person to be executed in over ten years in the state. Four shots were fired into a target pinned over his heart. Officially, the cause of death was execution by shooting - yet it can be argued that this was also an indirect suicide. It later prompted the New Wave popular music group The Stranglers to pen a cult record titled, Looking Through Gary Gilmore's Eyes.

Suicide has been around since the dawn of civilisation. Over the years, different religions have generally condemned the act, but to varying degrees. Ironically, though the Catholic Church views it in certain cases as a mortal sin, there are four suicides in the Old Testament. Samson and King Saul's are probably the most famous examples. Cleopatra used poison to kill her self. In the New Testament there is the suicide of Judas Iscariot. While neither the Old nor New Testaments specifically condemn suicide, it is contrary to the fifth commandment - Thou shalt not kill. The only exceptions to the rule would appear to have been in the case of martyrs, believed to have been divinely inspired in the pursuit of protecting the faith. In the Koran, the Muslim Bible, suicide is viewed as a crime worse even than homicide.

Yet suicide has not always been considered a disgrace. Among the Greeks and the Romans, it was held to be justifiable in certain circumstances. Roman citizens were allowed seek the permission of the Senate to take their own lives. However, this option was denied to slaves. Zeno, Eratosthenes, Cato and Seneca are on the roll of distinguished men among the ancients who took their own lives. Demosthenes, Mithradates, Hannibal and Brutus committed suicide to avoid capture by a foe. The ancient Greeks were very rational about it. According to the Greek philosopher Aristotle:

"To run away from trouble is a form of cowardice and, while it is true that the suicide braves death, he does it not for some noble object but to escape some ill."

Despite this considered view, in ancient Greece, the bodies of some suicide victims were buried outside the walls of the town with the right hand severed and buried separately.

The very fact that a person decides to end their own life, suggests that there was a time when life was once worth living.

The hardening of attitudes in the late Roman empire was partly due to the high incidence of suicide among slaves, as a result, depriving their owners of valuable property. Public attitudes towards suicide are still as ambivalent today as in ancient times. There have been apologists among the clergy and many eminent philosophers and writers have long argued the right to dispose of one's own life should one so wish. The great English dramatist and poet, William Shakespeare, managed to pack no less than fourteen suicides into eighteen of his tragedies among them Romeo & Juliet, Othello and Ophelia. Irish mythology also lends reference to suicide - Chuchulain went into his last battle knowing that he had lost his magic powers. In Irish literature Yeats's Deirdre of the Sorrow sells her soul to the devil and throws herself under the wheels of a chariot. In early Irish law, suicide was classified as fingal, a type of kin slaying. Suicide is barely referred to in the old law texts and it is likely that the suicide rate was genuinely low at the time. During the Elizabethan period, suicide was viewed as something romantic and dare one say, even fashionable. Indeed a certain romanticism has always surrounded the portrayal of suicide in fine art, literature and the theatre. The act of self-destruction stirs strong emotions such as fear, revulsion and recrimination. It is an ideal recipe for human drama. The Irish novelist and dramatist, Samuel Beckett wrote of suicide in Malone Dies:

"If I had the use of my body I would throw it out of the window."

In Victorian times attempted suicide was attributed for some curious reason to "silly girls and dragged hussies." At other times suicide would mean forfeiture of goods, and the burial could not take place on consecrated ground. While the early records of suicide are sparse it is known that the bodies of pauper suicides were dissected in anatomy departments for fifty years. In 1823 a man was buried at a crossroads in Chelsea with a stake through his heart for attempted suicide and the penalty of hanging for attempted suicide is even recorded in London up to 1860. In 1882, the practice of burying a person who committed suicide at a crossroads with a stake through the heart was prohibited. The Internments (felo de se) Act, 1882 stated that:

"It shall not be lawful for any coroner or other officer having authority to hold inquests to issue any warrant or other process directing the internment of the remains of persons against whom a finding of felo de se shall be had in any public highway or with any stake being driven through the body of such person."

The term felo de se, is the legal latin for suicide.
When the father of Irish Home Rule, Charles Stewart Parnell died in 1891 at the comparatively young age of 45, there were sug-

gestions that it may have been suicide. His grand-uncle Henry, who was also involved in politics, committed suicide in 1842. Parnell's affair with Kitty O' Shea had contributed largely to his downfall. The exact cause of his death still remains uncertain although when news of it became public at the time, there was much talk of a possible suicide; speculation which was even fuelled by Parnell's own mother. A post mortem was never carried out on Parnell's body - it was so hot, that it had to be speedily placed in a lead lined coffin. Poisons available at the time would easily have caused such high body temperatures.

The systematic collection of suicide figures began in earnest in the nineteenth century. The Encyclopaedia Britannica of 1911 noted the rise in suicide trends and drew attention to excessive rates in men, the old, the single and the lonely. This is still very much the case today. Attitudes to suicide became less hardened with passing years.

In 1926, the American journalist Alexander Chase alluded to the impact that suicide has on us all and perhaps the reason why it carries such a stigma:

"To attempt suicide is a criminal offence. Any man who, of his own will, tries to escape the treadmill to which the rest of us feel chained incites our envy, and therefore our fury."

At the beginning of the twentieth century, James Joyce offered a pragmatic approach to suicide in, Ulysses, his classic tapestry of Dublin life. Four men walking to a funeral begin talking about the subject:

"But the worst of all," Mr. Power said, "is the man who takes his own life." Martin Cunningham drew out his watch briskly, coughed and put it back.

"The greatest disgrace to have in the family," Mr. Power added. "Temporary insanity, of course," Martin Cunningham said decisively.

THE SILENT DEBATE

"We must take a charitable view of it."

"They say a man who does it is a coward," Mr. Dedalus said. "It is not for us to judge," Martin Cunningham said.

The British Suicide Act introduced in 1961 directed that a coroner's verdict of suicide would first need the full force of proof that the deceased had killed himself. A new phrase "suicide while the balance of the mind was disturbed" was developed by lawyers to protect against the crime of "felo de se" - one who kills - under which the property of the deceased reverted to the Crown. In Britain today, suicide and attempted suicide have not been criminal offences for many years. As in this country, however, it is a crime to enter into a suicide pact or to aid a suicide. Such an instance would be where a doctor gives a lethal dose of tablets to a patient, knowing they were suicidally inclined and intended to take them.

Over the years, society has viewed suicide in many different ways: first as a sin, then a crime; later in sympathetic light as result of social conditions and today more of a medical, social and public health issue. Thankfully, the penalties have become less severe. In the Isle of man in 1969, a court ordered that a teenager be birched for attempting suicide! The modern view is that suicide is due to a mixture of personal illness and a period of vulnerability. It rarely occurs out of the blue and warnings are usually given. As a general rule, the tendency to suicide increases with age.

During the nineteenth century social researchers commonly believed suicide to be a disease of civilisation. It appeared to be increasing in modern societies and absent in more primitive cultures. It is now accepted that suicide occurs in virtually all societies, although the rates vary considerably from one to another. French author and philosopher, Albert Camus, was fascinated at the rarity of suicide and posed questions still unanswered. His writings came at the dawn of scientific psychiatry, before the effective treatment for severe depression - the kind of illness that can drive some to suicide. Very depressed people feel worthless and alone; even in the midst of family and friends. The illness can cause extreme anguish and in this setting, successful suicide becomes almost understandable. But not all suicides have the link of a major depressive illness, especially when the victim is young. Disturbingly, it is among young men that Irish suicide rates are rising most quickly.

Some cultures have encouraged suicide, the most notable being the Samurai of old Japan. Hara-kiri traditionally was a highly-valued form of suicide committed to avoid overwhelming shame which usually occurred after an act of disloyalty or defeat in battle. Japan used to have one of the highest suicide rates but the act is now seen as less honourable. However, the number of suicides remains high in Japan today and a disturbing feature is the growing number of school children taking their own lives. Some of this has been blamed on bullying and exam pressures. Most suicides in Japan are by hanging and the most common reasons are illness and financial problems.

The suicides among the leaders of the recent failed coup in Russia are also of particular interest. Suicide can ensure that one does not fall into the hands of the enemy, alive. A suicidal soldier may also deliberately place himself in a position in which he will be killed by others during battle. This kind of behaviour would probably be indistinguishable from exceptional heroism. In other situations, suicide was and is still to this day inexorably demanded: the Suttee of the Indian widow forced to immolate herself by cremation on the funeral pyre of her husband or, in certain primitive tribes, exposure to the elements of the old and infirm and their abandonment. The Suttee disposed of widows for whom Indian society made no provision.

Suicide among the Eskimos relieved the tribe of the burden of an unproductive member. Very early records also show that widows committed suicide in North-West Europe immediately after the death of their husbands.

In pre-modern times, African tribes viewed suicide as evil and believed that physical contact with the body of a suicide would be disastrous. The tree on which a person hanged himself was cut and burned in order to please the ancestors and the place of the suicide was believed to be haunted by evil ghosts. For the Africans, suicide resulted in an earthbound ghostly existence.

Many forms of conventional suicide have since been abandoned. In India, the Suttee was forbidden by the British in 1828. Since World War II, ceremonial Hara-Kiri has virtually disappeared.

In Tikopia, a small island in the western Pacific where pagan ideology still lingers, the attitude to suicide is ambivalent. The Gods are believed to receive the souls of the dead but not of those who hang themselves. The Gods are not angered however if a man goes out to sea in a canoe to drown, or if a woman commits suicide by swimming out to sea. The Christian Tikopians believe that the soul of a suicide goes to Satan and not to paradise, a view not dissimilar from the Catholic church view in the past.

Buddhism is ambiguous about suicide. It is encouraged in certain circumstances - for example in the service of religion and country. For Hindus, death is not final, but rather a single incident in a lengthy series of existences. There still exists today what one could term as the kamikaze type suicide. A few years ago, a group of kamikaze bombers - fanatical Shia terrorists - drove trucks filled with explosives into the headquarters of the French and American peace keeping forces in Beirut. The suicide bombers killed 241 marines and 58 French paratroopers. In another incident a young suicide bomber blew herself up as she walked past an Israeli patrol in South Lebanon. Suicide bombers were also employed on the Iraq side during the Gulf War. In 1991, there was world-wide shock when the former Indian prime minister, Rajiv Ghandi, was assassinated by a suicide bomber, along with over a dozen other people. Evidence suggests that the female bomber had strapped plastic explosives to her body. The bomb exploded less than five feet from Mr Ghandi.

On other occasions, disturbed members of the public have gone on the rampage killing innocent bystanders, and eventually ending their own lives before being shot by police. The Hungerford massacre in Britain comes to mind as a terrifying example of murder followed by suicide. In all, 14 people were killed and 15 wounded when Michael Ryan went on the rampage putting a formerly quiet little town on the map and into the history books for the worst of reasons. In another recent case, a gas explosion caused by a woman trying to commit suicide, ripped through an apartment house in Italy and killed three people. The woman had been grieving over the death of her mother, turned on the kitchen gas and lit a cigarette.

Fanatical suicide for religious motives has also been exhibited until comparatively recently. In November, 1978, the world held its breath in collective horror when it learned of the mass suicide of 913 people in British Guyana, all followers of the People's Temple headed by Reverend Jim Jones. The cultists lived in an agricultural commune known as Jonestown. Survivors of the incident, later found hiding in the jungle, claimed that the cult's leader had forced his followers to drink a mixture of a soft drink known as Kool-Aid, laced with cyanide. A note, signed by Jones said that the deaths were an "act of revolutionary suicide." How he induced his followers to kill themselves remains a mystery. His own body, with a bullet in its head, was found among the corpses. The mass suicide was only discovered when the bodies of two American congressmen and five other people, who had gone to investigate Jones, were found near the campsite. Another mass suicide which went virtually unreported occurred in Vietnam in 1993. Over 50 hill tribe villagers in a remote Vietnamese hamlet committed suicide using flintlocks and other primitive weapons. It was understood to have been a case of exploitation by a blind local leader.

In the 1993 Waco massacre in Texas, 86 members of the Branch Davidian Cult died in an apparent mass suicide. The followers of leader, David Koresh are believed to have torched their compound after FBI agents used an armoured vehicle to inject tear gas into the camp. The tactic, which went horribly wrong, was aimed at ending a siege which lasted 51 days. A large number of young children also died in the disaster.

Within the Mafia families, a member who betrays his family, in a serious manner, is often expected to end his own life as an act of supreme recompense. This also ensures that his spouse and children, if any, are looked after for the rest of their lives and do not become outsiders. It also avoids the unsavoury prospect of the person having to be 'hit' by another member of the family.

The reasons for suicide can often be quite surprising. Recently in Britain, the connection between people accused of shoplifting and suicide has come to light. Each week, one person in Britain takes his or her own life after being arrested on a charge of shoplifting. The shame of being arrested for such an act is too much to bear for many.

A special organisation "The Portia Trust" has been established in Britain to help people in these circumstances. One couple, arrested for alleged shoplifting, were found in their family car having gassed themselves to death with car exhaust fumes. Before the suicide, the couple had wrapped up the family Christmas presents, paid all the household bills and made both their wills. In the car, beside the two bodies were two glasses and a half a bottle of sherry. The couple died holding hands.

One of the most prominent cases of suicide following shoplifting was that of Lady Isobel Barnett in 1980. A doctor, former magistrate and television star, she had been arrested for shoplifting a tin of tuna and a carton of cream worth 87p. Lady Barnett pleaded not guilty in court in the case which received worldwide attention. She was fined £75 for shoplifting.

"It was a horrible ordeal. I have only myself to live with and at least I can live with myself," she said after the trial. However, it was clearly a brave front on her part. Four days later, she was found dead in her bath, after taking her own life.

Personality, culture and individual circumstances are all important factors in a person's inclination towards self destruction. It has been suggested that some people may be born with a greater tendency to depression and therefore, a greater inclination toward suicide. Among the professional groups who care for potentially suicidal patients, suicide is known to be high among doctors, particularly psychiatrists, vets and dentists.

Today, suicide is a major problem in many countries around the world. Australia has the highest rate of young suicides and in America, rates have doubled. American investigators have pinpointed three key factors for the rise in suicides among young people; an increase in psychiatric risk factors particularly depression and substance abuse; a higher proportion of youth in society and an association between increased violent behaviour and access to firearms. Guns account for over 60 per cent of all suicides in America. As in many countries, there is disagreement in America over the factors for the rise in suicide. The American administration began an initiative to tackle suicide in 1992, headed by the Centre for Disease Control in Atlanta. The 'suicide programme' funds studies into copy-cat suicides that follow suicides by family and friends, or well-known personalities. However, the suicide programme has not been expanded by the current Clinton administration. As in Ireland, suicide is a sensitive subject and there are those who argue that asking questions about suicide will give people the idea to kill themselves. This is not borne out however by independent studies and such an approach appears to reenforce the taboo surrounding the subject of suicide.

Suicide is the third biggest killer in Australia, just behind heart disease and cancer. More Australians kill themselves than die in car accidents. The trend is blamed on high aspirations fuelled by the media, lack of confidence in the future, and the growing number of broken families. The high number of young people unemployed means that many will never work and will suffer the low self-esteem which possibly places them at risk. In Denmark, suicide has always been viewed as an individual's right and the country has one of Europe's highest rates. One of the reasons for this is honesty in reporting. There are strict rules on registering deaths and toxicological analysis must be performed if there is any suspicion that a person has taken his or her own life. This approach has brought its own problems with a drop in the Danish life expectancy. A Government group has been set up in Denmark to examine the problem and design a strategy on suicide. In late 1993, the Dutch parliament passed a new euthanasia law, by a small majority. While the law means that euthanasia and assisted suicide are still criminal acts and doctors can face prison sentences of up to twelve years, there are special guidelines which, if followed, prosecutions will not be taken. The guidelines direct that the patient must have expressed a voluntary and long-standing wish to die. Patients must also be suffering unbearably, with no hope of relief.

The process by which someone arrives at the act of suicide is difficult to examine, not least because they are dead. While suicide may often be as a result of a failure to handle the stresses and strains of life, there is a lack of consensus regarding the exact underlying psychological mechanisms.

Many factors influence a suicide: professional people commit suicide more frequently than those of lower educational levels. Suicide rates declined during the prosperous years of both World Wars but rose during the depression of the 1930s. Other factors which undoubtedly affect suicide rates include psychiatric history, depression, religion, age, sex and education. In the 1950s, studies suggested a link between suicide rates, especially in Europe, and times of war. It was argued that this was possibly due to social factors:

"Great social disturbances and great popular wars rouse collective sentiments, stimulate partisan spirit and patriotism, political and national faith ... and at least temporarily cause a stronger integration of society. As they force men to close ranks and confront the common danger, the individual thinks less of himself and more of the common cause." (Emile Durkheim, 1951)

SUICIDE IN IRELAND

There is evidence to support this argument. Attempted suicides dropped by nearly one third in Poland during the Solidarity crisis in 1981. In Northern Ireland in 1970, the suicide rate was half the annual rate of three years before the onset of the troubles. There has however been a large rise in the number of suicides among the security forces. In particular, many suicides have occurred among the Royal Ulster Constabulary, the most common method used - legally held guns. On the link between war and suicide, the British author and churchman, W R Inge wrote that:

"Hatred and the feeling of solidarity pay a high psychological dividend. The statistics of suicide show that, for noncombatants at least, life is more interesting in war than in peace."

It is clear that French sociologist Emile Durkheim, referred to earlier, also believed that vulnerability to suicide depended on the strength of bonds between the individual and society; the weaker the bonds the greater the risk. He noted the increased in suicide in industrialised areas such as inner cities where the cohesion of society was at it weakest. However, one potential flaw in his observations is his apparent failure to recognise the role of mental illness in suicide cases.

"The modern view is that victims (suicide) are caught in the crossfire between serious mental illness on the one hand, and extreme personal vulnerability at a point of time, on the other," consultant psychiatrist Professor Tom Fahy writes in his chapter on suicide in Colm Keane's revealing book, Mental Health In Ireland. "Contrary to popular belief, the suicidal state of mind is not something which persists over weeks or even days: the impulse comes on suddenly and does not last for long."

Durkheim believed that no-one would carry out an act he knew to be fatal unless he intended to die. Perhaps the most useful definition of a suicidal act then is, any deliberate act of self-damage which the person committing the act cannot be sure to survive. For example, someone who poisons himself with expert knowledge about the effects of a poison must be viewed in a different light to another who commits the act without such knowledge.

It was not until the early part of this century and the arrival of Sigmund Freud that suicide begun to be examined in more of a medical context.

Freud, however, was influenced greatly in his thinking by the devastation of the First World War - making him wonder about an unconscious death instinct in us all. His psychoanalytic attempts to explain suicide have not been widely accepted.

A person who commits suicide may not necessarily be mentally ill, although at least temporarily deeply disturbed. While religious beliefs may influence a decision towards suicide, the influence is rarely conclusive with respect to performing the act. Hungary, for example, a Catholic country, has a very high suicide rate. In most countries men commit suicide more often than women. In America, the ratio is about 3:1 although women usually make up two thirds of the suicide attempts.

In France, suicides are more common in rural areas, during the day, and at the beginning of the week. Suicides drop during the holiday season in July and August. Over 12,000 people died of suicide in France in 1989. The difference in lifestyles between men and women in France is particularly marked: men smoke and drink more than women, drive more dangerously and the suicide rate for men is three times as high as that for women. As a result there is a nine years life expectancy between the sexes.

One of the most popular methods of suicide in the West is the 'accidental suicide'. These deaths usually raise questions as to whether the victim intended to die by the act. The death of actress Marilyn Monroe is probably the most famous example. Although an autopsy showed that her death was caused by an overdose of barbiturates, investigators could not determine whether she intended to take a lethal dose. The question centred on the fact that people who take barbiturates sometimes become so drowsy that they are not conscious of how many they have taken - they

may also be unaware of the level of dosage that becomes dangerous. Many people still do not realise that taking a far more popular drug like alcohol can greatly increase the chance of a fatal
overdose.

A second common form of suicide is 'escape suicide', where
the victim sees him or herself as passing on to God. Philosopher
Frederich Nietzsche posed the question as to whether suicide is a
way out or a way in?

In the case of revenge suicide, notes are left behind often con-
taining statements such as "You'll be sorry for what you did" or
"It's all your fault". The author wishes to make others feel guilt
and responsibility for their acts. It is this type of suicide which
greatly distresses the family and friends of the deceased. Revenge
suicides are calculated to force others to feel the blame.

Some suicide notes are not quite so distressing - take, for
example, the brusque suicide note of the famous American inven-
tor and industrialist, George Eastman:

"My work is done. Why wait?"!

In reality, suicide notes are left behind in only a minority of
cases. While virtually unknown in this country, fake suicide notes
have also been written by people wishing to make a murder seem
like suicide. Others who wish to disappear for personal reasons,
leave signs that they may have committed suicide - but no body.
There have been a number of so-called 'Reginald Perrin' cases in
Ireland, where clothes have been found on beaches, but no traces
of a body. Suicide may be suspected but until a body is found,
either dead or alive, the case must remain open. Adults have a
right under law to disappear, although the falsification of a suicide
is a cruel act for the family and friends of the 'deceased.'

Those seriously intent on suicide will frequently take care that
they are not discovered. In cases where suicide notes are left, they
are rarely concerned with important matters. Usually they contain
reminders about where the car keys can be found; insurance policies; the location of the will and other practical matters - rather
than eloquent goodbye messages, as so often portrayed by cinema

and literature. In contrast, those who attempt suicide with no real intention of killing themselves are usually the ones who leave clues as to their intent, to ensure their action is suspected and that they are discovered in good time. Attempted suicide is in fact a misnomer, many of these people do not intend to die at all but are instead making a dramatic statement that they wish to change their life situation. Attempted suicide is often a plea for help.

Studies have shown that even psychiatrists who treat suicidal patients, often feel guilt when these patients kill themselves, although parents, lovers and others close to the victim are more likely to feel that way. In Ireland, so great has been the suicide stigma at times, that children of parents who have committed suicide have often had the fact concealed from them until they reached adulthood. The shock of such news in later life is one of devastation and, as in an Irish case dealt with later in this book, the trauma may contribute to severe physical disablement.

Accepting the fact that someone close has committed suicide is very difficult, for many, impossible. Consider the case of American actor Henry Fonda whose second wife, Frances, a manic depressive, locked herself in the bathroom and cut her throat from ear to ear. Henry Fonda found it impossible to accept the suicide and reportedly told his children Jane and Peter that she had suffered a heart attack. Jane Fonda learned of the true cause of her mother's death in a magazine she was reading at school while Peter learned about it from a newspaper article in Rome. He later went on a drugs spree.

While some may hide the fact that a suicide has occurred, others act to masquerade a murder as a suicide.

Consider the number of official suicides, reported by those Governments around the world, who have had a poor record on human rights. In Southern Africa, a large number of 'official suicides' among black people held in detention have been reported. These cases mainly stem from 1963, when legislation allowing imprisonment without trial was introduced. Of 29 cases examined by investigators, 20 were reported as 'suicide by hanging', five as 'suicides' and one as suicide by 'self strangulation'. The death of the Black civil rights activist Steve Biko in detention in 1977 was officially classed as due to a hunger strike. Evidence produced at the coroner's inquest however suggested otherwise. Scepticism about these suicides, among others, is heightened by the fact that some deaths in detention in South Africa have been listed variously as 'detainee fell ten floors'; 'slipped in shower'; 'fell from police car'; 'fell down stairs' and even - 'died of injuries'. Hopefully, the new post Apartheid South African Government will help to eliminate such events in the future. However, the annual reports from Amnesty International show that many such 'suicides' are a facet of daily life in many countries around the world.

There are many theories advanced to help explain suicide. Current research and thinking emphasises a mix of biological, psychological and social factors. Suicide may partly be explained by examining the changes that take place in people's circumstances and their reaction and interpretation of those changes.

For instance, some unemployed people may be more likely to commit suicide than others. But how many people interpret their unemployment as a depressed situation? Some just view it as a temporary setback, for others, suicide is a solution to their problem. A recent study in Cork has shown that a large number of suicides involved unemployed people. But the suicide link to unemployment may be different than first imagined. Those at particular risk would appear to be people in jobs who fear unemployment and those who have recently lost their jobs.

Depression is a common denominator among people who commit suicide. It may be a result of external events like a social situation, or organic in its origin. It is also a factor widely linked with homicide cases. A number of Irish cases on record show instances where a person decided to kill his or her family and then committed suicide. This is usually referred to as an extended suicide.

What motivates a person to commit or attempt suicide? From

talking to those who have attempted to kill themselves, many just intended to shock, anger or produce guilt in people around them. A small overdose of pills will usually have been taken, believing that it would not prove fatal and that they would soon be found. Others will attempt a kind of 'Russian Roulette' - their survival being placed in the hands of luck or chance. For example, a relatively small overdose may prove fatal because tolerance and reaction to drugs can differ from person to person. Yet, discovery may be delayed - a friend or family member failing to arrive at an appointed time.

A third group successfully kill themselves after considerable thought and preparation, many of the methods being extremely violent. In 1990, Patrick Sheehy, once described as Britain's most wanted man, was found dead with a handgun beside his body in Nenagh, Co. Tipperary. He was wanted for alleged IRA atrocities in both Britain and on the continent. According to the Garda forensic report on the incident Sheehy shot himself in the temple.

Poisoning through the inhalation of carbon monoxide used to be the most popular method of suicide. It is a simple procedure whereby the individual attaches one end of a hose-pipe to a car exhaust, puts the other end in the car and leaves the car running. However, the introduction of unleaded petrol and new car systems to reduce certain exhaust emissions has made this mode of death less attractive to some. Drug overdose, sometimes in combination with alcohol, has become the preferred method of the majority in many countries. In many cases, the drugs have been prescribed by a family doctor. The issue of over-prescribing by doctors is an important one with patients easily hoarding prescribed tablets. But, if prescribed medicines cannot be obtained from a family doctor for a suicide attempt, a proprietary medicine like aspirin or paracetamol will usually suffice and can easily be bought from a supermarket or chemist. Aspirin and paracetamol can have serious toxic effects on the kidneys and liver and are often more dangerous in the long term than drugs on prescription. Many people who buy medicines in supermarkets or shops over the counter just do not realise how dangerous these drugs can be in excessive dosage. Suicide cases involving poisoning present a particular difficulty. With other methods such as hanging, shooting, or jumping, the external appearance of the body will usually indicate that the cause of death was other than natural. If death was not expected an investigation will be called. The intentional self-poisoning of an elderly person with concurrent illness can easily be missed. This was highlighted in an investigation by N S. Patel who reviewed the findings of 15,000 autopsies which were carried out for technical reasons and where unnatural death was not suspected. He discovered that 764 of the people showed significant amounts of medicinal poison either in their stomach or their blood. His comments are interesting:

"The use of drugs requires no witness, they do not leave visible marks and present a picture similar to that of a natural death, the body being found anywhere in the house ... therefore the general practitioner when requested to call to attend the dying or dead patient has nothing to suspect and if the patient is dead, provided they are not surprised that the patient is dead, issues a death certificate without hesitation."

Sophisticated methods are needed to ensure that any fall in the number of suicides, especially among the elderly, is real or imaginary. This is especially important given the predicted rise in the number of elderly in Ireland over the coming decade.

Many of those who attempt suicide are already in contact with the health and social welfare services. Studies show that around two-thirds of those who attempt suicide consult their GP in the month before the attempt - making it vital for doctors to quickly identify those at high risk.

While the prediction of a suicide attempt is obviously difficult, the Irish figures suggest a greater need for doctors to be provided with increased training to detect suicidal impulses in patients and to take all suicidal thoughts and behaviour very seriously. Through careful questioning, some measure of the seriousness of an attempt can be judged. Yet some people seriously contemplating suicide will appear calm and detached. Among the possible questions which can be posed by doctors are: Do you ever wish you were dead? What have you thought of doing to get away from your problems? Have you considered harming yourself? It must be conceded however that impulsive suicides, those which take place under intoxication with alcohol or drugs, are difficult, if not impossible to predict or prevent through prior discussion. Some patients commit suicide despite exemplary medical care.

There are other serious questions which must be dealt with. Should seriously ill patients be allowed to die, when and how? What right has anyone to stop a person taking his or her own life? As Albert Camus, wrote in 1975 - knowing one has the power to end one's own life at any time, gives one the freedom to live. Moves to introduce voluntary euthanasia were first made over twenty-years ago in Britain. The 'suicide by proxy' Bill to allow people suffering from incurable illness to have their lives terminated painlessly, introduced in the British Parliament, was lost. Opponents objected strongly to what they viewed would be a new 'executioner role' for doctors. In America, 'living wills' have already been introduced whereby a patient instructs that their doctor end life support treatment if they end up in a vegetative state following an accident or illness. The American Supreme Court has accepted that it is reasonable to withhold life-saving treatment in some of these cases, which ended in the courts.

The 'Living will' is effectively an advance declaration, spelling out what a person wants done if they become too ill to state their wishes. The directive can ask that a doctor not provide unnecessary life-sustaining treatment, but it does not allow him or her to actively provide help to hasten death.

Recently, the Law Lords in Britain gave doctors permission to stop artificially feeding an unconscious patient. Tony Bland, the patient at the centre of Britain's first 'right to life' case was a young victim of the Hillsborough football stadium disaster. The five Law Lords ruled that doctors would not be acting unlawfully if they stopped artificially feeding Mr Bland. The case was one of the most emotive ever to come before the British courts.

The predicted increase in the number of aged in some countries, among them Ireland, along with medicine's ability to prolong life is likely to lead to calls once again for the legislation of voluntary euthanasia. In the Netherlands, for example, euthanasia accounts for nearly one in 50 of all deaths. A recent government commissioned report in the country showed that doctors complied with around 2,300 euthanasia requests and assisted with 400 suicides.

Passive euthanasia is practised in almost every hospital in Ireland on a daily basis without the existence of clear guidelines. A doctor's legal duty of care may include making a decision about the discontinuance of medical care in the comatose patient, where the benefits of so continuing are outweighed by the burden and the patient's right to die with dignity. It is permissible to relieve pain even if the drug dosages chosen have the effect of shortening life. Doctors are not engaged in prolonging life at any cost. But the issues now being raised are whether a doctor should be allowed or even forced to actively pursue death in the treatment of those suffering from a terminal illness or hopeless cases. This issue was central to the recent Dr Nigel Cox case in Britain. Dr Cox, a rheumatologist at the Royal Hampshire County Hospital, had given his long suffering patient, Lillian Boyes, a lethal dose of Potassium Chloride. Lillian had arthritis which caused such pain that she could not bear being touched. She asked Dr Cox to help her end her life. After her death, he was arrested, went to trial and was given a suspended sentence for attempted murder. He said afterwards that he did the best he could at the time. His motive was not to end Mrs Boyes life, but to bring an end to her suffering, he added. During the Cox trial a number of doctors and nurses stood in his defence. Some supporters suggested that his mistake was to record exactly what he had done in medical notes. In Britain, the Suicide Act makes it illegal to assist someone to commit suicide.

One person who has risen to world-wide prominence over his

belief that a doctor should be allowed to assist terminally patients kill themselves is Michigan pathologist, Dr Jack Kevorkian. He devised a 'suicide machine' to help people die. The poison injecting machine was transported around the US in a van. One of his machines involved a series of bottles connected to switches which the patient pressed. The first bottle allowed a harmless saline fluid to enter the bloodstream, a second released a sleep inducing drug while the third contained a lethal poison. The process only took six minutes. In 1990, Dr Kevorkian shocked the American public when he revealed that he had supplied this system to help a 53 year old mother to die. He was arrested, accused of murder but the charges had to be dropped under Michigan laws. He has since helped many more people to commit suicide. Dr Kevorkian has proposed that a new medical specialty be set up for 'Obiatry' - dying with the aid of a doctor. Dubbed 'Dr Death' by the media, Dr Kevorkian believes that helping people to die is in the best interests of society but his views and actions have brought him into bitter conflict with the law and the medical profession. He was struck off the medical register in 1992 and so he can no longer legally obtain drugs. This however has not prevented him transferring to the use of carbon monoxide in helping people die. He is currently facing charges of assisted suicide. The issues raised by the Dr Kevorkian case are ones which will increasingly face Irish society. The aim of the Voluntary Euthanasia Society in Britain is to make it legal for an adult suffering severe distress from an incurable illness to have medical help to die. The Society has proposed safeguards such as a second independent medical opinion, psychiatric assessment and consultation with nurses and family. Those opposed to such moves argue that doctors can make mistakes in terms of prognosis and new cures and treatments are constantly coming on stream. Also, new ways to relieve pain and new discoveries should not be ruled out. There must always be hope. One of the biggest concerns of all about so-called 'mercy killing' is, would euthanasia remain voluntary for long?

CHAPTER TWO

DISASTER IN SLOW MOTION

Suicide is on the increase in Ireland for a variety of reasons. It is the complex mix of these factors which makes tackling the rise in suicide so difficult. A good indicator as to why people feel suicidal, depressed or in despair is the profile of telephone callers to the Samaritans. The most common problems cited by callers to the Samaritans are loneliness, anxiety, marital and relationship problems, mental illness and bereavement. Money problems and sex-related problems also feature, but to a lesser degree.

There are things everyone should know about suicide, in particular, the 'at-risk' signs to be alert for in those around us we care for. These risk factors include a recent bereavement, marriage break-up or domestic violence; people experiencing health, employment or financial problems or drug dependency; and a suicide in the family or by a friend. Suicidal people often appear withdrawn and depressed and may find difficulty relating to others. They may even discuss suicide or death, or express feelings of failure or lack of self-esteem. People planning suicide often put their affairs in order and may even give away valued possessions. The suicidal dwell on problems that seem to have no solution, they may have no supporting belief or philosophy of life and may attempt suicide or self -injury. What can you do if you are concerned that a loved one may be suicidal? According to the Samaritans, you should show your concern and affection and get them talking about their feelings. Do not avoid the difficult subjects and show you want to understand. Do not try to cheer up the suicidal because the bright side you see may only make their darkness seem deeper. Do not criticise them or say what you would do or what you believe. Encourage them to seek help.

Irish society is facing more social unrest than before. Unemployment is high and the crime rate is increasing. For many, there is the dreadful prospect that they may never work in their lives. Unemployment and poverty can lead to psychological distress and severe depression, with a consequent risk of suicide or attempted suicide. However, it appears that unemployment has an unusual relationship to suicide. New information would suggest that it is not as major a factor as first thought. It seems that those at risk of suicide are people who have just lost employment, those under heavy pressure at work or people who have other employment worries - rather than the long term unemployed. The chronically unemployed appear to be at relatively low risk. Those who become unemployed late in life appear to be at particular risk. These areas are explored in more depth in a later chapter by Doctors Michael Kelleher and Patricia Casey. Other factors closely linked with suicide are depression, alcohol abuse, the illegitimate birth rate, financial difficulties, a fall in marriages, spiritual values and social isolation. Financial worries can be an important element. Some years ago, a Country Antrim family claimed that their daughter's financial crisis had led to her suicide. The nineteen year old girl had gone on a banking spree after she was awarded £5,000 in court damages for injuries following an accident. She spent her money on clothes, and a holiday in Tenerife as well as on her family and friends. While she thought that she had spent all the money in her bank account, £3,000 appeared in the account due to an error. A few months after she had spent the money, the bank claimed that there had been a mistake and commenced legal proceedings to recover their money. According to the family, under pressure to pay the debt and the interest due, she drove to a beauty spot near her home in Co Antrim and shot herself with her boyfriend's gun.

We must accept that since one can never enter the mind of someone who commits suicide, it is impossible to explain any suicide fully.

Why is there such a dramatic difference between the number

of men and women who commit suicide? Of the 354 suicides in 1992, men accounted for 296. It has been suggested that Irish society is failing to prepare men for the new challenges in life and, that women are better at coping. Irish society has certainly changed in recent years. Sex roles are no longer well-defined, women's role in society has been enhanced and the traditional role of men no longer exists. Unemployment has also deprived many men of the traditional role of bread winner which may be contributing to the crisis.

The official figures now show that we can expect 10 people in every 100,000 people to commit suicide in the Republic of Ireland. The attempted suicide rate is around 250 people in every 100,000. Our nearest neighbour Britain has a lower suicide rate while in Northern Ireland, the rate is even lower. Suicides in Northern Ireland have increased since the late 70s and early 80s with a significant shift to younger people and almost exclusively males. Doctors at Belfast's Mater Hospital, have found that the rise in suicides in Northern Ireland has been matched by a corresponding decrease in riots, bombings, and homicides. Although no direct connection has been made, this is interesting in the light of Emile Durkheim's remarks referred to earlier on war and suicide.

One of the big concerns about Ireland's suicide rate is that suicides among 15 to 24 year olds have increased dramatically. Particularly disturbing is the increase among young men in their late teens and early twenties with no obvious psychological illness. While suicide among the very young is thankfully quite rare in this country, this author is aware of the case of a twelve year-old girl who killed herself with her father's shotgun because of a bad school report. The Institute of Guidance Counsellors has warned that suicide threats are increasing among school pupils in Ireland. The reasons may be low self-esteem, peer pressure, parent pressure, academic pressure and even bullying. There is a concern that some bright teenagers may make a suicide attempt out of anger or impulsiveness, making this group a difficult one to treat. The Institute says more psychologists should be appointed to second level schools as the existing service is very overstretched. Suicide among young children is a sensitive subject, and little information is available. There can be little doubt however that a single suicide within a school can traumatise other pupils. Four children between the ages of 10-14 are believed to have committed suicide in 1990. Some psychiatrists are concerned about instances where children run in front of cars and are either killed or injured. Suicide cannot be ruled out in all cases. For parents, this is a difficult topic and an emotional minefield.

It is known from research that Irish children often think of killing themselves. Of 50 children who attended a child psychiatric out-patient clinic in Dublin, 15% said that they had though of killing themselves but had not made an attempt; 8% had made a suicide attempt. All the children who had attempted suicide knew someone who had attempted suicide. In a second study of suicidal thoughts in adolescent girls in an inner city school in Dublin, nearly 7% often thought about killing themselves and 22% sometimes think about killing themselves.

Consultant child psychiatrist Dr Michael Fitzgerald, who was involved in these studies says that suicide is rare among children under 12 years of age. Among child psychiatrists, there is much controversy about the concept of a depressive illness occurring in children. Some would question whether very young children are actually able to make judgements about their feelings and behaviour.

"In most of the attempted suicides among children, drugs are involved. Overall, we must be careful of overestimating the extent of suicide in this country. While I accept the findings of the major suicide studies in Limerick, Cork and Galway, we should be careful about extrapolating nationally, figures from small studies in single counties," Dr Fitzgerald advises. He estimates that the actual number of people who commit suicide in Ireland is around 20% greater than the official figures. The fact that schoolchildren commit suicide suicide may be linked to bullying. The Irish school's Stay Safe programme deals with the issue of bullying and the

problem is now being confronted in the modern educational system.

Children as young as seven have been admitted to Dublin
hospitals after deliberate overdosing on drugs. Aspirin and paracetamol are among the most common drugs used along with sleeping pills. A family argument appears to be a common denominator
in terms of precipitating an overdose. It must be emphasised however that only a very small number appear determined to kill
themselves. The Poisons Information Centre at Dublin's Beaumont
Hospital reports that over 3,300 enquiries a year involve children
under nine years of age, most of these appear to be accidental poisonings.

If we add to the national suicide figures those who are
believed to attempt suicide every year - it is clear that what we
are witnessing is a substantial group of people in need of special
care.

The political battle to force a change in the law making suicide no longer a crime has been a long and hard-fought one. The
person most closely associated with this campaign is Limerick
Senator and Fine Gael member, Dan Neville. It all began at a small
and unexceptional young Fine Gael meeting in Tralee in November
1990, attended by around 20 members. A FG member from Clare,
Seamus Mulcanny proposed a motion that "Young Fine Gael calls
for the immediate decriminalisation of suicide and the setting up
of a task force to tackle the mounting problem of youth suicide."
The motion was passed and aroused particular interest in Dan
Neville.

"My first cousin died by suicide as did one of my close
friends. Nobody is untouched by suicide. I placed a motion on the
Seanad Order paper in January 1991 calling on the government to
decriminalise suicide and to set up a task force to tackle the growing problem. I failed to get a debate on the motion. Later in June
of that year, I published a Private Members Bill, the Suicide Bill
1991," he explained. This short Bill proposed that suicide should
cease to be a crime and provided for criminal liability for complici-

ty in another's suicide with a maximum 10 year sentence on conviction.

The Bill was introduced by Fine Gael on its own private members time in November and December, 1991. However, the then Minister for Justice, Mr Ray Burke (FF) promised to introduce a similar bill before Christmas. As a result, the government parties voted down Dan Neville's Bill.

Earlier, the underreporting of Irish suicides was officially acknowledged in the Dail in November 1990 by the former Minister for Health, Dr Rory O' Hanlon. The Central Statistics Office, he said, estimated that official suicide figures were understated by around 15-20%. However, Dr O' Hanlon refused calls for a special commission to be set up to examine Irish suicides, arguing that there was no evidence of any marked worsening of the problem. He told the Dail:

"It is generally accepted that there is some under-recording of the number of suicides in Ireland, as in many other countries. However, media reports that the real suicide rate may be very much greater than that shown in the official data are not borne out by recent studies with which the Central Statistics Office has co-operated.

"These studies suggest that, in the areas studied, the official statistics understated the number of suicides by at most 15-20%. Discussions are taking place between my Department, the Department of Justice and the Central Statistics Office to consider the feasibility of any changes in the reporting arrangements which might help to increase the accuracy of the official statistics.

"Statistics published by the World Health Organisation show that Ireland's suicide rate is among the lowest in the European Community. There is no evidence of any marked worsening of the problem and I do not consider the establishment of a commission or a review group to be warranted at the present time.

"The causes of suicide are complex. Changes in the cohesiveness of society, depression, and an erosion of traditional values, a lack of employment opportunities and social isolation are all factors which can contribute to individual distress."

During this Dail debate, Dr O'Hanlon was challenged by the then Fine Gael health spokesman Ivan Yates, who claimed that there had been a significant increase in suicides in the Waterford area, especially among young people. Nine young men from Waterford had drowned in the same stretch of the River Suir in the space of a few months during the year. While claims were made that the deaths were associated with demonic possession and drug gangs, no concrete proof to support these allegations was presented. It has also been alleged that the deaths may have been the result of what is often referred to as a suicide 'copycat' syndrome. In the majority of the cases, the pathologist's report showed that a small amount of alcohol had been consumed by the young men.

Ivan Yates also asked the Minister if he was aware that the annual reports of a number of Irish coroners had suggested that "deaths have been recorded as misadventure and so on when they were suicide cases." Dr O' Hanlon reiterated that the evidence suggested the level of underreporting to be very small. He said that there had been a substantial increase in the number of recorded suicides since 1970 but that this was because Ireland had a low base to start with.

Before a Committee of Public Accounts in 1991, Cork TD Bernard Allen called on the Government to decriminalise suicide. He claimed that in some cases Gardai were not inclined to record a death as suicide because it would label the deceased as a criminal. In response, the director of the CSO, Mr Thomas Linehan said that the figures which his office released were around 80% correct and talks were continuing with the Departments of Justice and Health to obtain more accurate information on the problem.

The political debate on the issue has been confused. Mrs Mary O' Rourke, the successor to Dr O' Hanlon as health minister in late 1991 said that contrary to media reports, the official statistics in Ireland did not substantially understate the actual rate in Ireland. Since these speeches were made however, the figures for more recent years have become available and show a definite worsening of the problem.

Dan Neville's campaign continued. Padraig Flynn had replaced Ray Burke as Justice Minister and the suicide legislation promised was weeks overdue. The issue was raised in both the Seanad and the Dail by Fine Gael and others but with little success. As a result, Senator Neville published a new Private Members Bill, the Suicide Bill 1992. This was a more comprehensive document than the earlier one. It sought to maintain the ban on a Coroner's jury publicly considering the question of suicide, but allowed the Health Minister to set up a scheme whereby information on the social aspects of suicide could be gathered by the Department of Health and made available to *bona fide* researchers on an anonymous basis. This was a more adventurous Bill aimed at obtaining better records of suicide in Ireland. It was particularly progressive in the view that a kind of social post-mortem should take place to establish the causes and trends in suicide. However, it too fell in November when a general election was called. During this period, Dan Neville was a regular voice on radio and television, keeping the issue of suicide in the public eye. He also met and corresponded with leading researchers here in the area of suicide, including Cork consultant psychiatrist, Dr Michael Kelleher, (who is conducting a major research project on attempted suicides in the Cork area), UCD Professor of Clinical Psychiatry, Prof Patricia Casey, and Galway consultant psychiatrist, Professor Tom Fahy. "I was annoyed at the way the issue was being treated from a political perspective. For political reasons, the government would not accept a private members bill in the Seanad," Dan Neville says. Undeterred, he re-published his Suicide Bill and it was introduced by Fine Gael at private members time on 28, April 1993. However, on the morning of that day, a new sense of urgency gripped the Government and Justice Minister, Maire Geoghegan Quinn introduced a Bill in the Seanad, similar to Dan

Neville's. She asked that he withdraw his Bill as she had published her Bill and she would be asking the Whips of the Seanad to arrange widespread support to decriminalise suicide. In a surprise move, the Justice Minister introduced her Bill in Dail Eireann in May 5, 1993, and so the government parties in the Seanad voted to remove the Bill from the Seanad. The Minister's Criminal Law (Suicide) Bill passed into law a short time later. Since the law change, Dan Neville has remained relatively silent on the subject. It is not due to a loss of interest, but rather an effort not to become too identified and labelled as the 'suicide senator.' However, he is anxious to be involved in promoting suicide prevention programmes and remains unhappy with some of the terminology still associated with suicide. In particular, he dislikes the term "commit suicide" as the word commit has an association with criminal acts.

Recently, the Democratic Left party proposed that the Irish Government set suicide targets, and try to reduce the number of suicides by 20 per cent by the year 2000. According to the party, this reduction could be achieved by training doctors to be more aware of 'suicide signals'. Their programme would include better education for family doctors and funds to allow cases of major depressive illness to be treated in general practices, with special attention to high risk groups. The British government has already set itself to reduce the number of suicides. Other countries, such as Holland, have gone even further with special lectures to secondary school students on suicide and depression. This approach is controversial and some believe counterproductive by placing undue anxiety in the minds of children.

The Department of Health had been examining the establishment of a confidential reporting system for suicides, whereby two sets of deaths certificates would operate. This was before suicide and attempted suicide were decriminalised. Under the system, a 'public' death certificate would not mention suicide but a separate 'confidential' certificate issued by coroners to the CSO could include such a verdict. However, the concept had its problems.

There was concern that having a suicide recorded on a confidential document was risky from a legal viewpoint, as coroners at the time were not allowed to record such verdicts. Also, given the potential for a court to order the production of these confidential certificates at some stage, their confidentiality could not have been guaranteed. Eventually the idea was scrapped as it was seen as a legal minefield.

A second suggestion aimed at recording suicides by other means also fell through. It was proposed that statistics could have also been gathered from coroners by telephone. In this case, department officials felt that such statistics would have been virtually unacceptable in an academic sense. The official view was that if a suicide recording system was to operate, it had to be an open one. Clearly, the onus was being shifted to legislators to change the law, rather than administrative procedures.

Comparing Irish suicide figures with other countries is not as straightforward as it might first appear. The manner in which official suicide statistics are gathered and presented differs greatly from one country to another. If the figures are artificially low, as is the case in Ireland, comparisons are virtually meaningless. According to the World Health Organisation:

"The true incidence of suicide is hard to ascertain. Varying methods of certifying causes of death, different registration and coding procedures, and other factors affect the extent of completeness of coverage, making international comparisons impracticable."

In addition, we have no machinery for officially recording attempted suicides, a problem more widespread than suicide itself. Were such a system were to be introduced, it would most likely only offer a 'best estimate', as cases of attempted suicide not admitted to hospital or seen by a doctor would not be recorded. In cases of attempted suicide, there is much collusion by survivors, family members and friends to cover up such incidents. It is estimated that each year the number of attempted suicides in Ireland each year could be between 8,000-9,000.

Even comparing suicide studies from different regions around Ireland throws up contradictions. A study of suicide in the Galway area in 1978 found a suicide rate of 13 for every 100,000 people compared with the CSO's 5.8 for the area in the same period.

Under British law, for coroners to record a suicide verdict, it must be proven that the deceased initiated actions that lead to his own death and that he did so with the express intention of causing his death. There must be evidence of intent before a suicide verdict can be returned. As we have already seen, relatives of the deceased in Ireland can appeal to the courts against a verdict of suicide. In Britain, this was originally done for financial reasons because in a suicide verdict, the deceased's property had to be surrendered to the Crown. Today, appeals are made for reasons of sensitivity as the old penalty no longer exists.

Such an appeal occurred in 1975 in England involving a man who it is believed either fell or jumped from a building. The coroner's verdict was suicide, because the circumstantial evidence led him to the conclusion that the deceased intended to kill himself. However, the appeal was permitted, and successful, because it was felt that no direct evidence of intent was shown.

Twenty years ago, Irish suicide rates were very low. Studies at the time indicate that the rate was genuinely low. Suicide was largely confined to elderly people, recently bereaved, often those who were physically impaired or depressed. Changes have taken place since then resulting in a largely unexplained increase in suicides. The profile of those who commit suicide is also changing and we need to discover why.

A recent study of suicides in County Limerick showed a suicide rate, two and a half times the national rate. The study, conducted by Dr Peter Kirwan, consultant psychiatrist at St. Joseph's Hospital in Limerick, involved a survey of local coroners who were asked in which inquest cases they would have returned a verdict of suicide, had the law permitted them to do so. It revealed 11 suicides from a population of over 60,700 for the year 1989. The cases involved; five hangings, two poisonings from weedkiller, two carbon monoxide poisonings from car exhaust fumes, one drowning and one electrocution. These findings raised questions about other studies which had drawn links between suicide and unemployment and marriage breakdown, an indication the difficulties we face trying to examine the causes of suicide. All but one of the suicides in the Limerick study involved employed people and the majority of them were married. One of the group was a woman and the average age was 45 years. While the numbers involved in the study are small, the results are interesting.

"The study adds further weight to the view that the official suicide figure greatly underestimates the true state of affairs assuming that the population (of Limerick) is representative of the country as a whole," Dr Kirwan says in his report. "If it is the case ... that there is an increased risk of suicide in those exposed to suicide, then the need for a specific therapeutic out-reach response becomes all the more urgent, as does an end to the legal anomaly whereby suicide remains a criminal act." Since publishing his 1989 study, another confirmed case of suicide has been returned by the coroner for the year in question and the law has been changed.

The majority of those who kill themselves are still elderly, socially isolated and depressed. Given that a dramatic increase in the number of elderly people is predicted in Ireland over the coming years, urgent action is needed to stem the tide of untimely deaths. The increase in the elderly population here will be greatest along the Eastern seaboard area, particularly in Dublin. Suicide among the elderly often attracts little public attention, an indication that perhaps the death was understandable and due to the problems many people face in old age: bereavement of a spouse, failure to adjust to retirement, physical illness often resulting in admission to hospital and the psychological pain of loneliness.

The profile of those who actually kill themselves is very different from those who attempt to do so - although there is obviously some overlap. More women attempt suicide than men. Many patients admitted to hospital following an overdose do not express a wish to be dead when interviewed by doctors. It is grim to note, however, that many of those who attempt suicide will try again and succeed within a year of the original attempt. These people are most at risk in the first week after the original suicide attempt. One of the tragic consequences of attempted suicide is that many who take this course subsequently end up hospitalised, some with major injuries. As a result, the vicious circle of depression continues and these people are now at an even greater risk of committing suicide.

We have seen how over three times as many men kill themselves than women in Ireland. The methods used by men are usually violent, punitive and brutal. Spring and Summer are the most common times for suicide. The Christmas and New Year periods are also a time when certain people are at particularly high risk. The late Dublin City coroner, Dr P J. Bofin found the Christmas and New Year seasons very disturbing due to the dramatic increase in number of people who called to his surgery complaining of depression and expressing suicidal feelings. It is a trend paralleled in admissions to hospital casualty units which also peak dramatically around Christmas and the New Year. Those in need of company look for solace and friendship in hospital wards. It is a time when people recently bereaved can feel most alone. It is also a period of great tension among families as they come together in a concentrated form. Most of us have experienced the dramatic surge in rows during the so-called season of goodwill, often influenced by an overindulgence in food, drink and too much leisure time. There has been much comment and conjecture on what are the 'facts' concerning suicide in Ireland. Let us look now at the figures that are available, and what they tell us.

NUMBER OF 'OFFICIAL' SUICIDES NATIONALLY
(1980-93)

1980	216
1981	223
1982	232
1983	282
1984	232
1985	276
1986	281
1987	262
1988	263
1989	252
1990	311
1991	318
1992	353
1993	169* (by mid-year)

Total Number	3,670 suicides

Cork has been identified as one of the country's 'suicide blackspots'. In the Southern region between 1979-86 the number of suicides increased from 40 to 67. A substantial amount of work in researching suicide in this part of the country has been conducted by Cork consultant psychiatrist, Dr Michael Kelleher and Dr Maura Daly.

Their investigations found that between 1980-85 a total of 149 men and 58 women killed themselves in the Cork area. Most suicides among men were due to drowning or hanging. Only 15 of the men involved took overdoses. Most of the men who killed themselves were unemployed at the time. Hanging was more common in rural areas and drowning in urban areas, probably due to ease of access. In the Cork area, a particular bridge over the River Lee became the site of a series of 'copycat' suicides among young men - all known personally to each other. In the case of the women, hanging was not a popular method - over half of the women chose drowning as their means of suicide.

Self-poisoning alone in Cork City costs the health service in excess of £500,000 a year. The cost of a day in casualty is in the region of £200. From a national perspective, self-poisoning and suicide is costing the Irish health service millions of pounds each year.

The method of suicide chosen will depend on what is both available and what is acceptable. In most rural areas, there is easy access to lakes, pools and streams. Likewise, in country areas, guns are more common, used principally by farmers for pest control or at shooting competitions. As a result, suicide methods used by people living in towns and cities compared with their country counterparts will usually differ. In Waterford for example, a study found that half of suicides were due to drowning, reflecting the access to river and sea in the county. In Kildare, where the rates have doubled, suicide among men is usually by hanging or shooting while among women, the method chosen is usually drowning.

In his book, *Can we prevent suicide?* New York author David Lester makes an interesting point about the effects of gun control laws on the incidence of suicide.

"The impact of strict handgun control statutes on suicide rates have convinced me that restricting the methods available for suicide will have an impact on the suicide rates."

His view is similar to remarks made over one hundred years ago by William Farr: "In certain states the mind appears to be fascinated ... by the presence of a fatal instrument ... and the withdrawal of the means of death suffices to save the life." According to Dr Tom Fahy, Professor of Psychiatry at University College Hospital Galway, the official Irish suicide rates should be doubled or quadroupled to give a true rate. A couple of hundred suicides, he says probably "conceal a true rate of about 1,000 annually." It remains unclear as to how much the official figures now reflect a true rise or a greater readiness by the Central Statistics Office and others to enter suicide as a cause of death.

There can be however, no questioning the number of suicides in Irish prisons, reported with tragic frequency in recent years. The suicide rate in prison is around four times the rate in the rest of society. Around half of prison suicides occur within three months of prisoners being remanded in custody. Many involve prisoners who have been involved in violence in their family circle. The recent Advisory Committee on Prison Deaths report found that 17 of the 23 suicides examined over a 16 year period were as a result of hanging from cell window bars. It recommended new safety standards including specially designed windows. Other problems in prison, contributing to the problem, include over-crowding, the need for improved medical and psychological services and improved assessment of prisoners when first committed. An international report has pointed to the lack of adequate suicide risk prevention measures in Irish prisons and the level of medical care. The report followed an inspection of prisons here by the Committee for the Prevention of Torture (CPT), a body attached to the Council of Europe. It also noted the dispensing of drugs and medicines by untrained prison staff and the treatment of prisoners with mental disorders. The Committee visited Mountjoy and Wheatfield in Dublin, Cork and Limerick Prisons and St Patrick's Institution in Dublin. Despite the recommendations contained in the Whitaker Report into prisons, a medical director of prisons was not appointed until late 1990. Some time later, following a spate of prison suicides, extra medical orderlies were appointed to all of the country's closed prisons and special suicide review groups were set up to single out those prisoners most at risk. The early warning system is still in its early days. However, in recent times, prison officers have however been able to foil a number of attempted suicides by prompt action. Prisoners are vulnerable and may easily feel threatened by other prisoners' words or deeds. As regards those imprisoned for paramilitary activities, the comrade-ship of the men and women in such movements appears to sustain them.

One of the most highly publicised prison suicides of recent times was that of 19 year-old Sharon Gregg in Mountjoy Prison. She was the first woman prisoner to have committed suicide in Ireland in living memory and was serving a twelve month sentence for larceny. It is understood that the rope used by Sharon Gregg to hang herself was made from strands of wool which had been obtained in the prison knitting class. Her last poem, written in Mountjoy, read:

"I don't want to become bitter
And filled with hate.
I've seen too much hate
I don't want to be angry any more
Forgive me please for what I have done
And help me to live right again"

Many other prison fatalities were equally disturbing. Twenty three year-old, John Patrick Buckley was jailed for life in 1989 for murder. The jury at his trial rejected a plea that he was insane when he strangled and stabbed Breda Hanrahan in his flat in Ballybunion, Co Kerry earlier that year. He claimed that he could kill again and had given himself up to the Gardai so that society would realise that he was dangerous. He said that he had killed Breda Hanrahan so that he could have sex with the corpse.

At Buckley's trial, the jury heard conflicting evidence from consultant psychiatrists. Two were convinced that he was psychotic and suffered from a mental illness yet to be classified. Two other psychiatrists concluded that he was not legally insane.

In December 1989, Buckley - sentenced less than one month previous to life imprisonment for murder - was found hanging in his cell in Mountjoy Prison. His death provoked an outcry from many quarters with calls from the Prisoners' Rights Organisation for a public inquiry into what they said was an alarming increase in the number of deaths in Irish prisons.

DISASTER IN SLOW MOTION

An angry Senator Joe Costello of the PRO commented that despite numerous recommendations in recent years by coroners at inquests, no steps had been taken by prison authorities to prevent access to prison bars, the most common means of self-inflicted deaths in prisons. Following Buckley's death, the then Fianna Fail-Progressive Democrat Government set up an inquiry into prison suicides which has since reported.

It is clear that poor conditions, overcrowding and inadequate medical facilities are contributing to suicides in Irish prisons which could be prevented. Prison officers are also concerned that in the future they may become subject to litigation from relatives claiming negligence in such cases.

While the Department of Justice denies that it has a policy of settling compensation claims brought by relatives of prisoners who commit suicide, it is understood to have paid out £7,500 in 1990, in the case of a Mountjoy prisoner who died from a self-administered overdose. Sometimes, it can be easier to obtain drugs inside an Irish prison than in the open community.

While few investigations into prison suicides are available, an Australian study found that in a consecutive series of 44 deaths of male prisoners in Brisbane maximum security prison, 20 were due to suicide. Over half of these suicides took place within the first two months in custody and those on remand were more prone to commit suicide than were sentenced prisoners. A history of psychiatric disorder was common and 40% of the prisoners had previously attempted suicide. Hanging was the most common method used in the prison suicides.

Increasingly, the Irish courts are having to deal with people who require more extensive medical and social care in Irish prisons. Despite the large number of prison suicides, the number of suicides in psychiatric hospitals is even higher than those in prison here. There have been over 60 suicides in psychiatric hospitals here since 1987, despite the existence of special observation units.

The progressive closure of a large number of psychiatric beds in Ireland is a matter of major concern. One only has to look at the large number of admissions and attendances at psychiatric clinics and hospitals as a clear indication of the toll of stress in Ireland. Over one in ten admissions are on an involuntary basis.

Recently, there has been a policy shift in the Department of Health from hospital-based to more community based care for certain patients. This is a worthy development as long as the facilities are in place to cope with the change. Some doctors are concerned that dangerously-ill patients are being released onto the streets and may be ending up in the prison system as enough money has not been provided for alternative community based care.

In a highly publicised case, a woman patient was sent to a Dublin Mental Hospital after she committed murder when she was discharged from a psychiatric hospital in another part of the country. Each time she had been discharged, her condition worsened. The woman, who was a severely disturbed schizophrenic, eventually committed suicide in a Dublin Mental Hospital in 1990. She had torn a strip of fabric from the hospital bed linen and used it to hang herself. In the case referred to, there was no evidence from the patients' behaviour or condition to suggest that she was at risk of suicide.

Is there a way in which medicine can, through the use of drugs, prevent suicide attempts? At Trinity College Dublin, scientists have been researching a new drug to combat overdoses by patients suffering from depression. The drug which the researchers believe may help patients recover from an overdose of anti-depressant tablets, has yet to be produced. Overdoses on antidepressants are a serious problem since patients being prescribed the drugs are those most likely to take overdoses. In the studies at TCD, the aim is to produce antibodies which will bind with the overdose drug in the body tissue and induce it back into the bloodstream. The team, headed by Dr Clive Williams, are looking to develop a range of novel antibodies that can bind to the 'overdose' drug and pull it out of the tissue.

"All of the technical work has been done but the project has been on hold for some time as we seek support for the project from the pharmaceutical sector," Dr Williams said. Producing an antidote drug to combat the overdose drug is technically very difficult. The antidote drug will need to be around one hundred times more powerful than the overdose drug. This kind of research has obviously far-reaching implications. Around one in ten drugs prescribed to medical card holders in Ireland are tranquillisers. With drug poisoning, coroners are more likely to give an accident or undetermined verdict rather than in other cases of self-inflicted deaths. Research is also underway to discover why people who commit suicide are lacking in serotonin in their brain. These studies may lead to identifying potential suicide suspects. There is evidence to suggest that biochemical levels in the brain may affect a person's tendency to suicide or acts of extreme violence. Antidepressants operate by affecting the levels of chemicals such as noradrenaline and serotonin within the brain. These chemicals are neurotransmitters, passing between nerve cells carrying impulses from one to the other. Some of the drugs are more sedative than others. Lithium, for example, is used to treat patients with mood swings from depression to schizophrenia. Since the early sixties, the sedatives, Librium and Valium have been widely available to treat tension and anxiety. A wide range of anti-depressant drugs and sleeping pills are also on the market, some have been the source of much controversy.

Around 15% of people who suffer from severe depression at any time will commit suicide. The risk is greater when a family member or acquaintance has already committed suicide - sometimes referred to as a 'suicide gene' in a family. Ireland has twice the British admission rate to psychiatric hospitals. Acute psychiatric hospital admissions in Ireland have increased in recent years. In 1991, there were 27,913 admissions to Irish psychiatric hospital and units a slight increase on the previous year. The highest number of admissions ever recorded in any year was in 1986 and the trend, though high, has been dropping ever since. Men have a higher admission rate than women, the largest number are among the widowed. Most admissions are in the 35-44 year age group.

Depression disorders account for the greatest number of admissions to psychiatric hospitals followed closely by alcohol abuse and schizophrenia. Most of those admitted for depression are women, while those admitted for alcohol or schizophrenia are men. Unskilled manual workers are up to six times more likely to be admitted to a psychiatric hospital than employers or managers. For the spouse of a person admitted to a psychiatric hospital following a suicide attempt, life can be very difficult. The spouse may be blamed for 'driving' the husband or wife into hospital. A lack of support for the family of a person hospitalised following a suicide attempt has been highlighted in letters I received during my research for this book. One letter said:

"My wife was admitted as a patient to a psychiatric hospital. She is an alcoholic and had attempted suicide. I found that there was tremendous sympathy among the staff towards the alcoholic, but little towards me. While my wife was in hospital, I had to cope with the family and as I was self-employed, my business suffered. There is plenty of counselling for the patient in hospital, none for the family affected. Some of my neighbours, through their comments, appeared to suggest that I had driven her into hospital."

One of the more hopeful signs however is that first admissions have decreased with an increase in re-admissions and that voluntary admissions have more than doubled in the last forty years. While 88% of all patients who enter psychiatric hospitals do so on a voluntary basis, 12 per cent are involuntary admissions. This percentage is high by international standards. It is important that depression should not be used as a 'catch-all' explanation for suicides. In Primo Levi's dramatic account of life in Auschwitz, *The Drowned and the Saved*, he reveals that suicide was virtually non-existent in the Nazi concentration camps. Can one imagine anywhere more depressing than Auschwitz? Primo Levi committed suicide, but it was in 1988, a long time after his tragic war experiences.

Apart from high-population areas like Dublin and Cork which have a very high number of suicides, a number of other counties are also reporting large number of suicides. These include, Galway, Donegal, Kerry and Clare.

Suicides and undetermined cases, by County for 1990*

COUNTY	TOTAL
Leinster	
Carlow	5
Dublin county borough	51
Dublin Belgard	5
Dublin Fingal	6
Dublin Dun Laoire	13
Kildare	11
Kilkenny	4
Laois	2
Longford	2
Louth	5
Meath	10
Offaly	3
Westmeath	9
Wexford	11
Wicklow	9
Munster	
Clare	14
Cork county borough	12
Cork county	34
Kerry	14
Limerick cnty Borough	5
Limerick county	13
Tipperary Nth	2
Tipperary Sth	10

Waterford county borough	2
Waterford county	11

Connacht

Galway county borough	5
Galway county	22
Leitrim	2
Mayo	10
Roscommon	7
Sligo	3

Ulster, part of

Cavan	4
Donegal	14
Monaghan	4
Totals:	334

*For 1990, the latest figures available from the Central Statistics Office, on breakdown by county.

MOST COMMON METHODS OF SUICIDE IN IRELAND

Men	*Women*
Hanging	Poisoning
Drowning	Drowning
Poisoning	Hanging
Guns & explosives	Gases
Other gases and vapours	Jumping
Jumping	Other means

DISASTER IN SLOW MOTION

The most recent Dublin study of suicides has shown that the average age was 41 years but ranged from 17 to 78. This is in keeping with the trend in recent years in Western Europe of an increase in the number of young males taking their own lives, according to Drs Sheila McGauran and Michael Fitzgerald, who conducted the study. The most common method of suicide in Dublin was hanging, followed by self-poisoning. Drowning was the third most popular method employed.

Over half of the Dublin suicide victims in the study had been in contact with doctors in the month before their death. Over a third had expressed thoughts of suicide and over one quarter had taken action in anticipation of death - making or changing a will, or leaving a suicide note.

Evidence of a feeling of hopelessness was found in many of the cases, a feeling well-documented as a psychological precursor to suicide.

It is clear that a national study of suicide must be undertaken, supported by the Government and if possible the European Union. Local Irish studies can have local biases and at times some studies here appear to contradict eachother. A national study would pull together the strands of local studies and give us a better picture as to the real level of suicide in Ireland.

CHAPTER THREE

THE PERSONAL TRAUMA

On a subject such as this, there is nothing that can quite match human testimony. In early January 1994, as part of the research for this book, a notice was placed in the national press in Ireland asking people to write of their experiences regarding suicide or attempted suicide, among their families or friends. A similar announcement was made on RTE radio, courtesy of *The Pat Kenny Show*. It was agreed that all correspondence would be treated in strict confidence, with the sensitivity required and that permission would be sought prior to publishing any personal stories. The level of response to the request was quite astonishing and the nature of the replies were both deeply moving and in some cases, very disturbing. Some of those who replied revealed that it was the first time they had written in detail of their personal trauma regarding a suicide. Others remarked that the more outspoken people become about suicide, the less shaming it is for those left behind. I am deeply indebted to those people who took the time and courage to write and discuss events of such a personal nature. What follows is a series of personal stories, selected from the large public response. Other stories, which I chose not to publish, proved invaluable for my research. For reasons of confidentiality, certain names, dates and places have been changed, but the events remain true. I have tried to keep to the original words and text supplied, where possible.

John

I met John, my husband, when I was 16. We both came from similar backgrounds so there was an instant attraction. He was a heavy drinker even then, but I did not see it; he was good and kind. We married in 1974, I was just 20 and he was 24. Our first son was born a year later, David in 1980 and our daughter in 1988.

Our married life revolved around John's drinking. It began with him gradually going to the pubs after work, progressing to not coming home at all until the early hours. I spent my married life alone and I used to cry a lot. Yet I always believed John when he said that 'tomorrow' would be better. In 1979 he was admitted to hospital for alcohol addiction. After that, the next ten years were spent going from one doctor to another, hospital to hospital, believing each time would be the last and he would be better. His sobriety from alcohol by this time had led to drug dependency and I lived with the fear of not knowing what to expect from one day to the next.

I would go to work in the morning leaving my troubles behind and then dread having to face returning home in the evenings. I can see now it was a terrible way to live but hope always kept me going. It was not until February of 1989, before our daughter was a year old, that I suddenly reached the end of the road and could take no more. It took a lot of courage for me to ask John to leave because I did not believe I could manage without him, a part of me still loved him and I did not want to let him go. When he moved into a flat in the town I was very hurt; I had felt deep down that he would see what he had, what he was doing to himself, get the help he needed and come back to us. I had isolated myself for many years and had no close friends, so I was very lonely and I did not talk to anyone.

The last time I saw John was in his flat in October of 1990. I had met him the previous weekend on the street. He had crashed two cars shortly before that. I stopped to talk to him and he was very upset. He was crying and said he was trying to get in touch with his own doctor because he had ran out of pills and needed something for the weekend. His doctor was not on duty so he had asked the chemist for some drugs and was going to pick them up.

I drove him to the chemist, waited and brought him back to his flat. I was very concerned and wanted to bring him to hospital but he told me he was okay and wanted to do things his way.

So, I left him and returned to see him the following Monday evening. He was back to his old self. When I questioned him about seeking help he became very angry. My last words to him were that I did not want to see him again. I saw him only once after that, as he was walking towards his flat. We did not look at eachother. The next time I saw him was in a coffin.

In December 1990, he was found dead. He had told his friends and those who shared the flat he was living in that he was going to Dublin. He had put away his car, locked his front door and bedroom and had taken an overdose of tablets. Nobody knew he was at home. He lay unconscious at the side of the bed where he had fallen, dressed in his pyjamas. The electric blanket was on, he had even failed to make it back to his bed.

The owner of the flat became worried when John failed to contact him for a week. He decided to break down the front door and discovered the body. It was the flat owner and a local priest who came to tell me the dreadful news at work. I will never forget it. Having to tell the boys was terrible. They had received a letter from John just a week earlier and they thought he was in Dublin.

We had just done our Christmas shopping that weekend in Dublin and John's name came up a lot, as we thought he was nearby. His was the first present the children bought. The funeral was a very lonely time for us. John's family blamed me for his death and kept away from us. I laid him out at home for the boys to say goodbye in the privacy of our own home; it was a good decision. They needed this time to be with him and accept his death. Coming home from the graveyard with just myself and the boys, my sister and her boyfriend, was very sad and lonely.

When I look back on it now, I do not know where we got the strength from to cope. I admire my boys very much today for their courage and dignity. These memories are still very painful to remember. It took a long time before we could say the word 'suicide'. The memories of our last angry words tormented me for a long time. I was angry with John and deeply resentful towards him for leaving me with such tortured memories. I would see him lying on the floor where he had lain for five days before being found, wishing I had called. I tortured myself with 'if only's'.

It was two months later that I was introduced to the bereavement counselling services in our local area. This is a structured support programme for widowed/separated people enabling them to work through their grief towards a new beginning. This was my first step towards recovery but more important, it was my first step towards personal growth. It focussed my thoughts for the first time on examining myself. The suicide group started a year later. This is where families and friends who have lost a loved-one by suicide come together to share experiences and this is where I was first able to say the word suicide. I could talk about my anger and feel the love and understanding from others in the group. It gave me the courage to face the pain of loosing John through suicide and for me the pain has been my healer. I was able to talk to my children and today we can talk honestly about his death. I took my eldest son to one of the meetings and he cried for the first time for the Dad he lost and more especially, for the Dad he did not know.

All of us have grown with love for one another and respect. My youngest son and daughter have taken part in a programme for children who have lost a parent and although my little daughter is too young to understand, my son David was able to tell his story for the first time and this has been great healing for him. I am still involved in the suicide group because without the support myself, I would not be living today. I have made peace with John. The memory of the loving man I lost years ago to his addictions, has come back to me and now I feel at peace with him and myself. I have been able say goodbye to him and lay him to rest with love and understanding. He will always be part of our lives but now I remember him as the husband I once knew, and not the man who died alone in his flat.

Kevin

In October 1992, I attempted suicide. How I survived, and why, is a mystery to me. I do not presume that I am any more important than the next person but somewhere in the scheme of things, I seem to have been given a second chance in life at the age of 47.

As an only child in a comfortable home, I was subjected to hours of drunken waffle from my father. I learned to bottle-up the fear, anger and hatred of this torture. Also, for as long as I can remember, I stole things I wanted, sneakily and cunningly when the opportunity presented itself. In a lifetime of dishonesty, I have rarely been caught.

I received a good education and did quite well with a minimum of effort. On being 'let loose' to university, totally immature and irresponsible, I had no direction or goal in life and tried to enjoy my freedom. After a few aimless years, I ended up in a good job, met a girl, fell in love and without any proper thought, got married at the age of 23. I took my first drink on the second day of our honeymoon. Marriage very quickly lost its sparkle for me as drinking and gambling became the only loves of my life. I suppose my ability to bury emotions, my wife's strength of character and a basic like for eachother contributed to us remaining together for 25 years - not all of it bad. We have three good children, who thankfully have not been too affected by my drinking.

I drank as I stole, sneakily and alone. Most of my friends never knew I had a problem, I did it so successfully. In almost 25 years of steady, progressive drinking, there were a few mortifying events to arrest the downward slide. I managed to remain in work and embezzled enough money to keep my family reasonably okay and myself drunk by bedtime each night, in order to sleep. In the months leading to the 'explosion' as I call it, my appetite had gone, the shakes were getting worse and I knew my health, job, marriage and sanity could not last. I was convinced that there was nothing I, or anyone else, could do about it. So, these thoughts and feelings were stored away with the rest of the negative experiences in an overloaded part of my mind.

I can honestly say that to everyone except my wife, who admits that she never really knew me, I am a friendly, good humoured, dependable, likeable all round nice person, and a good worker too. My wife caught glimpses of the sick person I really was inside, and I believe it had a profound affect on her, more than she perhaps realises. I really wanted peace and contentment in my mind, but it seemed getting drunk was the only anaesthetic from the pain. I never seriously considered suicide as a way out, but in the early hours of that fateful morning in 1992, a combination of circumstances came to a head. After a drunken row, my wife became the focus of all my anger and resentment. Revenge was the motive for my actions, until I was actually sitting in fumes in my car in a remote place and realised what I was doing. There I believe the safety-valve blew and let loose all the stored up garbage in my head. I gulped down a half-bottle of vodka and passed out wondering where I was off to. I never once thought of the pain I would leave behind. Two and a half hours later I was found in the car with a still-running engine. I was 'pumped' back to life, and suffered a broken rib in the process. It was recommended after a period in a psychiatric hospital that I attend Alcoholics Anonymous. I was mentally and emotionally numb and it took quite a few meetings for my mind to grasp any sense of what was being said and to realise that I was truly, an alcoholic.

It is now one and a half years since my last drink. I find this unbelievable given that I considered myself to be so weak. Life is infinitely better in every way. It was not easy at first and I have been through the pain of a necessary - for me - separation from my wife. The compulsion to take a drink does not strike as it used to, all possible due to the fellowship of the AA. I unloaded my mental anguish onto the ears of other understanding recovering alcoholics. The release from guilt, fear and loneliness is hard to put into words here, as is my gratitude. Countless small, but important events have occurred out of the blue. I got another good job which I believed would never happen after what had occurred in my last post. The ability to fall asleep with a peaceful mind is more valuable than any wealth. I consider myself a novice with so much more to learn.

Most important of all, I have discovered a loving God who I ask to be my manager each day, as he sees fit. He has not let me down yet.

Martin

My father was 69 years old and had been suffering from a heart complaint for some years. Being a very nervous man, he was reluctant to enter hospital for proper treatment. His own doctor prescribed tablets for his ailment for around four years but it was only after his death that the family discovered he had given up taking his medication around nine months earlier.

He was a man who never had much faith in medicine and I suppose he thought the tablets were having little effect. I believe he never quite came to terms with the fact that he was ill, having worked very hard all his life as a small farmer and cattle-sheep dealer. Towards the end, he was practically sitting out his life in front of the fire.

My mother and he lived comfortably with no money worries and all of the family within a few miles. There had been a family fued for around eight years after my sister married a nice man, but one who did not ' fit the bill' because in my parents' eyes, he was not good enough for their youngest daughter. My mother never accepted this new arrival into the family fold. However my father saw that he was a good husband and made my sister happy. My father was willing to have him visit the house at any time. I suppose my mother was very stubborn and it certainly added to my father's depression.

My father had some land partly let to a cousin but a nearby farmer had been pressing him about renting this land. Both the cousin and farmer began fighting over the issue. My father did not wish to give his neighbour the land but at the same time he did not wish to offend him. He had been a good neighbour for many years. However, the cousin had been practically reared by my father and was always there when hands were required for hay-saving, lambing and other jobs. One day, the neighbouring farmer telephoned my father and asked for a definite yes or no to his offer. My father agreed to meet him. However, after his usual breakfast, he went for a walk and did not return. He was later found in the fields. He had taken a small dose of strychnine which proved fatal. His manner that morning was normal and he spoke to two people who said they could not see anything unusual about his manner.

I had my suspicions about his death almost immediately but it was nearly three weeks before the Gardai confirmed the result of the post-mortem. Breaking the news to my mother, my wife and my three sisters was the hardest thing I have ever had to do. Now, nearly two years on it still keeps me awake wondering how he could have taken his own life. My mother is only now beginning to go out again and this is only due to the great family and neighbours which have all rallied around her. My oldest sister had some professional therapy and is now doing quite well. I and my other two sisters are very busy with work and our own families and with the help of our partners - who are brilliant - are managing to live with this terrible tragedy. I will always ask myself why? Perhaps if we had all been more firm with him about having hospital treatment?

Anne

I was attending seven day school in fifth year in the 1970s and was doing fine with no obvious problems. However, things started to go wrong and I suffered a nervous breakdown at the age of 17. I had to spend two weeks in a local psychiatric hospital where I received electroconvulsive therapy, ECT. After the two weeks, I was discharged and returned to school in September to study for my Leaving Certificate. Having been put on medication in the hospital, I felt very dopey and lethargic and showed little interest in my studies. Concentrating was difficult. I had a very good sense of humour prior to my illness, but after my breakdown I was a completely different person. I stuck it out as best I could until November came and I became very disillusioned again and depressed. I skipped school for around three weeks. However, somehow, despite the problems, I completed by Leaving Certificate and did well considering the little effort I was able to put into study.

After secondary school and my exams, I got a job in a hospital. I was working there for two weeks but became unwell again and was admitted to a local psychiatric unit. The difference between this hospital unit and the last was that it was less strict; patients' doors were not locked. During this time I felt a great cloud of darkness which prevented me from seeing reality. I began to despair of ever getting better and saw myself as being of no use to anyone. It seems strange to speak of such feelings at the age of 19. Yet, as the days passed by, I began to think of suicide. I wrote a letter to my parents telling them how much I cared for them. I posted the letter, left the psychiatric hospital and made my way down to the town. My reason for doing what I did next was not to die, I actually wanted to live but only if I was well. I was not afraid to die because I had told God that I was going to him where I could be with him and help others through my constant prayers in heaven. I certainly felt that I was going to a better place.

It was a late autumn evening. I climbed onto a bridge in the town and jumped into the river below. My only recollection is that as soon as I hit the cold water I was back out again, surrounded by Gardai. I was taken back to the hospital and remained there for around two more weeks, before I returned to work.

I did not regain my health for some years after and I am still on prescribed drugs. However, at the moment, things are fine and I have a good job.

THE PERSONAL TRAUMA

Peter

My father Peter committed suicide around five years ago. He was an alcoholic who abused myself, my other brothers and sisters, physically, sexually and mentally. He was a man of high professional standing but who hated his job, married and felt he had too many children. There were 11 children in our family.

My mother and he appeared to spend most of their married life unhappy, fighting and using the children for their own purposes. My father suffered from depression and was given early retirement. He began drinking even more and went down hill fast. My mother eventually left him, as he would not leave our house.

My father deteriorated rapidly, rarely ate or washed, but just drank. His mother died around this time. He travelled to the funeral in the West of Ireland where he was born and he stayed in the family home until his death. Before he died, he was still drinking heavily. One night, he drove to a quiet place in the mountains and placed the hose from a hoover on the exhaust and into the car. He was found the following morning. My mother denies the fact that he committed suicide. She says that the car broke down and he put the hose on the exhaust and fed it into the car to keep himself warm.

I was glad and felt a sense of relief when he died. I only wished he had done it years ago. I was in my twenties when he died and so by then, the damage had been done.

Alan

My brother Alan committed suicide over ten years ago by hanging himself. I was living in England at the time and gave up everything to come back home after the event. My brother was only 31 and he suffered from a speech impediment. He had to take a lot of abuse because of his ailment and the curse of unemployment did not help either. He was a highly intelligent and sensitive person, who did not drink or smoke. He lived at home with my parents, who were both in their seventies. After Alan's death, none of our lives were ever the same again. There is not enough help for the people left behind following a suicide. I recall vividly the Sunday we had to travel to the mortuary to collect his body. Some children made up a joke and ran up to tell me. I felt sick. Worse was to come. Those who had tormented my brother began to follow me, even in my pain. However, I stood up to them. I also felt that the local newspaper was insensitive in its handling of the inquest. I went to the inquest in place of my parents.

Alan had a great love for horses and music. He would never have known how to hurt anyone. The year he died, there had been 13 suicides in six months in our town. Apart from his interest in looking after horses, Alan was in the folk group and the Civil Defence. There was a large turnout at his funeral and he was well liked, except for the ignorant who scoffed at his speech impediment.

The pain of loss following a suicide is indescribable. It never goes away. There are so many unanswered questions. And while there were people who were insensitive to Alan's plight, there were also many good people too. I recall going up to the park where he had taken his life. The spot where he had died had been defaced. As a result, I could not leave a bunch of flowers at the site and returned home.

Dermot

Life had no meaning anymore for my brother Dermot, when he took his own life in 1992, on a gloomy and miserable day. The weather seemed to reflect his mood. He was just 25 years old. Dermot took his car out and drove onto a dual carriageway in Dublin. He stopped the car, connected a hose from a hoover to his exhaust pipe and sealed up his doors and windows. He switched on the car and waited for his life to end. According to the Coroner, he died from carbon monoxide poisoning. As the song goes, suicide brings many changes. Life has its ups and downs for most of us, but we tend to come through the dark tunnel of depression to the other side, feeling we have survived. Yet, there are people who never come through this tunnel. For these people, they may feel the only way to resolve a problem is to give up the most valuable thing they possess - their own life. It is a sad and lonely individual who plans his own end. Perhaps Dermot did not consider the effect his death would have on our parents, the family and his friends, who were left behind to pick up the pieces of a shattered life. The mayhem, destruction and horror of his death has left a scar that will never heal. A pain so deep it has no end. Was it a selfish end, a courageous end or a thoughtless end? Denial and a feeling of shock, guilt and anger were all part of the grief reactions that I felt when Dermot died. He was the youngest in the family and so much of all our love was given to him. But it seems this was not enough to save my brother. It just leaves me and my family members with a powerful sense of failure. It is still very hard for me to say the word 'suicide'; yet I know it is important to speak of it to allow the healing process to continue. I felt guilty for a long time after Dermot's suicide, however I know this is a normal feeling. I also know deep in my heart that it was his decision, not mine. There is always a need to ask why someone committed suicide, although in Dermot's case there just is no clear answer. I will probably always struggle with the question why. The realisation that I will never see Dermot again is hard to accept. It is difficult to adopt a positive outlook on life again, especially when everyone around you is feeling low. I knew that resorting to drink or drugs to help me through was not the answer. I took up new pursuits, to try and gain strength. Grief is painful but coping is essential for one's own mental and physical health. Acceptance is the first step towards coping. Asking questions such as 'why' does not help. The other important step in coping with a death by suicide is seeking professional help. Family and friends can help you to pick up the pieces. It can take years before a suicide is seen in perspective. My one message to those affected by a suicide is, make yourself better not bitter.

Paddy Doyle, Author

Irish author and disabled activist, Paddy Doyle, has lived a life paved with tragedy and trauma. Although his condition was medically diagnosed in 1961, doctors knew little about it. He spent ten years in Irish hospitals, underwent brain surgery at the age of nine and was examined by numerous doctors.

"I was always amazed that the state never arranged for people to visit me, especially as I was being operated on in hospital and it was they who had placed me in care."

The circumstances of his father's death in 1955, by suicide, just six weeks after his mother had died from cancer, became known to Paddy only when he was 35 years old. Following the death of both parents, he was separated from his sister. An Irish court directed that he be detained in an industrial school in the care of nuns in Waterford, under the Children's Act 1908-41. A gripping account of his experiences is detailed in his award-winning book, *The God Squad.* At the hands of his carers, he suffered both sexual and physical abuse. Gradually, his left foot began to turn in. He later lost the use of both his legs and became permanently disabled. The cause of his rare condition - generalised idiopathic torsion dystonia - is unknown, although there are indications that it may have been trauma induced. Paddy was just four years old when his father committed suicide. Apparently, he witnessed the suicide and was found wandering around his father's farm eight hours later in distress. Only in recent years was he able to confirm the actual cause of death after scouring local newspapers in the National Library for details of the incident.

"The coroner's death certificate states that my father died from asphyxiation due to hanging. There is no mention of suicide. People did not mention how he had died at the time. Personally, he died when I was 35 years old, the time I discovered the real circumstances. I still do not know where he is buried as he was placed in unconsecrated ground. I have no photographs of him either."

Paddy believes that if the doctors who treated him in hospital had been made aware of his father's suicide, then their approach to treatment might have been significantly different.

"I was always suspicious that something had gone wrong with my father. Apparently, as a child, I spoke incessantly of seeing my father hanging but the nuns would not permit me to talk about it. If you don't discuss something, how can you purge it from your system or understand it?"

Paddy believes that Irish people should address the issue of suicide for what it is.

"We must accept suicide as a fact of life. We cannot go about hiding and disguising it as something else. If we fail to recognise the problem, how can we have realistic support systems for those who are affected by it." It is also wrong to assume that all those who commit suicide are insane, he argues.

"I do not say this just because of what happened my father. It is wrong to suggest that everyone who commits suicide is mentally imbalanced. Some people plan their suicide with great calculation and precision. It is a handy excuse for society to describe people who commit suicide as insane - an excuse to be shut of the problem."

Paddy continues to write and now lives in Dublin with his wife Eileen and their three children.

"Eileen has never read *The God Squad*, she finds it too disturbing. The man she knows now is not the child in the book. How I survived the experience without bitterness remains a mystery. Obviously I did a lot of mental bridge building over the years."

CHAPTER FOUR

ON THE FRONT LINE

We may all be more aware of the risks of suicide among those around us, but this has not resulted in a drop in the number taking their own lives. The professionals on the front line who have to deal with suicide cases on a daily basis include priests, gardai, coroners, family doctors, psychiatrists, psychologists and the social services. All signs of suicidal intent must be taken seriously. Yet, a small number of people continually threaten suicide as a means to manipulate others to their own ends. Identifying who is at risk and who is not is a very difficult task. The fact that around ten in every 100,000 people will 'officially' commit suicide in Ireland each year makes intervention most difficult. Following a suspicious death, there are certain criteria which the authorities take into account to decide, on balance, whether it was by suicide. These criteria include: the presence of a suicide note, intimation of intent prior to death, does the mode of death suggest suicide and are the circumstances suspicious. If notified of a suspicious death, the State pathologist may be called to investigate. He makes his way to the local garda station for a briefing. The pathologist may view the body if it is still lying where it was found. Other bodies will already be at the hospital mortuary. The pathologist will consult the Gardai about the circumstances and assess timing of death from examining the body. A preliminary report on the nature of the death may be given to the officer in charge. A written report is then later sent to the gardai and the coroner.

Doctors differ in their approach to dealing with people at risk of committing suicide. Severe depression is a state in which a person is most likely to seek to bring about their own death. Yet, can all those who commit suicide be viewed as being mentally ill? The

74

moraes of a society influence the attitude to the act. Certain medical conditions also play a part. Schizophrenics, epileptics and
those high on drugs are at high risk of committing suicide. Among
Irish schizophrenics, drowning is the commonest method of suicide. Most have been admitted to hospital on numerous occasions
and have been involved in previous acts of deliberate self harm.
But where do we class the Jehova's Witness who refuses a vital
life-saving blood transfusion on religious grounds?

With almost all physical illnesses, patients will seek cure or
relief from a doctor, but with mental illness things are very different. Doctors hold varying opinions as to when a depressed patient
should be admitted to hospital. Some believe that careful consultation with a patient will often elicit an outpouring of suicidal
thoughts. It is strongly advised that suicidal patients be prescribed medication in small amounts, with a ban on alcohol. If
possible, a trusted friend or relative should dispense the tablets.

Other doctors insist that even in cases of serious depression -
where there is not as yet any suicidal intent - sound reasons often
exist for admitting a patient to hospital. Dealing with depressed or
suicidal patients has its risks. One Irish consultant psychiatrist
took to arming himself with a shotgun and hatchet after threats
from some of his patients. In one case he was threatened for 18
years by a psychopath who was planning to infect him with a
virus. The patient eventually hanged himself.

Doctors are taught that every patient with an emotional problem, no matter how apparently trivial, should be assessed for suicide risk. Even patients who have never attempted suicide are
asked whether they feel hopeless or blame themselves for their
problems. However, the most difficult patients to help are those
who impulsively attempt suicide, without any warning.

But is it fair to expect a family doctor to take complete
responsibility for the management and care of a suicidal patient?
After all, these patients have such a variety of ways readily available to them - rivers, ropes, shotguns, weedkillers, medications -
that twenty-four hour supervision and observation is often

required. But is it feasible? Recently, both hospitals and doctors have been held liable for a lack of care in not protecting patients from the risk of self-inflicted injuries. In Britain, a hospital was held negligent for not having a constant watch on a patient suffering from a dangerous condition, who jumped from a window. Another hospital was cleared of negligence when a female patient, with suspected suicidal tendencies, eluded the nurses and went home and killed herself. In 1981, the controversial British judge Lord Denning ruled that there was no liability where a patient who had attempted suicide after treatment severely crippled himself. Such actions had to be discouraged, he argued.

In another case, a Dublin woman took a High Court action against St James's Hospital claiming that she was seriously injured in a suicide attempt after she was allegedly refused a bed in the psychiatric unit. Psychiatrists are particularly difficult to sue successfully because of the nature of the specialty. Unlike in surgery, there are no real physical results to observe following treatment. Psychiatry too, like all professions, has its bad apples. In 1981, a psychiatrist in Britain who mixed socially with a female patient was held to have acted in an undesirable way. He had known that the patient had fallen in love with him. She suffered a deterioration in her mental state and had attempted suicide.

A number of court cases claiming negligence against Irish psychiatrists are pending. Suicide and attempted suicide represent one of the most common reasons why psychiatrists are being sued by relatives and friends. Bad medical records or a psychiatrist's failure to obtain a patient's records from his or her previous hospital is useless as a defence for being unaware of a previous suicide attempt.

Among the factors which will determine whether a doctor was negligent are: whether the doctor foresaw the suicide, if he provided reasonable care and took reasonable precautions. Studies show that doctors themselves are a high risk of suicide. Psychological problems begin early in doctors' careers and many medical studies report emotional distress. Overwork, limited social life, constantly breaking bad news and failing to cure patient all contribute to the risk. The increasing number of complaints against doctors is also a growing worry. For a psychiatrist to have one's patient commit suicide, is similar to a surgical death on the operating table. Every day, health professionals have to face patients who have attempted suicide or successfully killed themselves. Ironically, the strain it places on members of the profession also makes them highly vulnerable to suicide. It has been claimed that the suicide rate among Irish doctors may be four times as high as members of other professional groups. Unfortunately the data complied in Ireland on suicide does not detail deaths by profession, so this is not easy to verify. It is known however that suicides among doctors generally, are carried out quietly. There are few doctors who attempt suicide. Erratic hours as well as the high emotive involvement of physicians when treating patients contribute to the strain. With recent cuts in the health service, some doctors, particularly GPs, have been under heavy financial pressure.

The cliche that doctors do not get involved with patients is untrue. For psychiatrists especially, a suicide often represents a failure to treat the patient successfully. A special Sick Doctors Scheme has been in existence for many years to help members of the profession who need medical assistance, usually for alcohol or drug related problems. It is probable that the suicide rate among doctors is influenced by their very accessibility to the most common method used by them - drugs. Another vulnerable group are farmers who work under great financial pressure and the constant fear of failure. Farming is a solitary profession, heavily dependent on seasonal factors. It is a solitary profession which attracts little sympathy from city folk. For farmers, there is an easy of means to suicide - shotguns and open water. Irish vets are also highly prone to suicide because of the stress in the profession, long working hours, usually without the support of an assistant. In 1990 there were six suicides among the country's veterinary surgeons. While there are no figures on the main professions at risk in Ireland, a recent British report of suicides by profession shows the top ten to be:

1 Vets
2 Pharmacists
3 Dentists
4 Farmers
5 Doctors
6 Therapists
7 Librarians
8 Typist, secretaries
9 Social scientists
10 Chemical scientists

Many complex dilemmas face doctors on the issue of suicide and attempted suicide. Should a depressed patient be given information on the toxicity level of certain drugs? By bringing up the very subject of suicide, could doctors inadvertently be planting the suicidal thought in the patient's mind ? Yet against this, there is the fact that a person's understanding of the lethality of a drug is an indicator of the seriousness of planning and intent to kill. The Samaritans say that from their experience, asking questions about suicidal feelings will not give the person the idea.

Should all 'suicidal' patients be placed in hospital and would we have enough beds for them? The number of long-stay beds in psychiatric hospitals has been reduced in recent years.

Mental health legislation in Ireland, relating to the detention of patients in psychiatric hospitals, needs urgent updating. The laws under which we currently operate were drawn up in 1945. Under this legislation a person can be committed to a psychiatric hospital by a relative or someone other than a relative, like a Garda, if necessary. The head of the psychiatric unit must sign the patient in and a consultant must sign the order for committal. Many doctors now believe that with so many voluntary admissions, patients should be allowed to give 72 hours notice of leaving a psychiatric hospital. A patients' continuing detention would be certified by a consultant psychiatrist and confirmed within two days by a second opinion, it is proposed. A decision to detain a patient on an involuntary basis would be made by a consultant psychiatrist, who would detail his reasons for so doing. His decision would be reviewed within two days by a second opinion. While the period for continued detention would be around 28 days, a review group of medical, lay and legal opinion would review the requirement for detention within seven days. Any extension past 28 days would be reviewed by a court. Overall, the proposed change would ensure that detention is required in the first instance and on a continuing basis. With the danger of Ireland being brought to the European Court of Human Rights over its outdated mental health laws, the Department of Health is planning to change existing legislation. Attempts to introduce new legislation to replace our old mental health laws failed in 1981 because of flaws in the draft bill.

The recent abortion controversy in Ireland and the ensuing Supreme Court judgment has also opened up a minefield for health professionals, especially psychiatrists in the area of suicide.

The decision of the Supreme Court in *Attorney General v X* and others (March 5, 1992) affirmed the right of a mother to a medical termination of pregnancy where, as a matter of probability, there was a real and substantial risk to her life if the pregnancy continued. The case involved a 14 year old alleged rape victim who had reportedly threatened to commit suicide unless she could have an abortion. The decision, which attracted world-wide attention, angered many psychiatrists, one of whom declared the judgment medically unsound. According to Dr Patricia Casey, Professor of Psychiatry at University College Dublin, the judgment ignored the impact of treatment of a suicidal patient.

"As far as I am aware, there has never been a case in Ireland where a termination of pregnancy would have been recommended by a psychiatrist as part of the treatment of a suicidal patient," she said at the time.

SUICIDE IN IRELAND

The prediction of suicide is a particularly difficult area. In the case before the Supreme Court, evidence that the girl was suicidal had been given by a psychologist. As the specialists most qualified to determine whether a threat of suicide is real or not, psychiatrists are likely to carry the burden of the court judgment. It is claimed that women who have suicidal tendencies are actually safer when pregnant and that hormonal changes in the body during pregnancy guard against psychiatric illnesses. Other doctors believe that, even if the number of cases where a pregnant women may be at risk of suicide due to her being pregnant is likely to be rare, these cases must be catered for.

In March, 1993, the Irish Medical Council, the policing body for doctors here, issued controversial new guidelines on abortion which stated:

"While the necessity for abortion to preserve the life or health of the sick mother remains to be proved, it is unethical always to withhold treatment beneficial to a pregnant woman, by reason of her pregnancy." The Health Minister, Brendan Howlin asked the Medical Council to clarify its position following the publication of its guidelines. At its annual general meeting in 1993, the Irish Medical Organisation voted by a majority of 102 votes to 45 to reject abortion. The Government has still to decide if, when and how it will deal with the substantive issue of abortion and the matter of suicide. The Irish Medical Council guidelines to doctors on abortion were published in the new ethical guide for the profession in 1994, unchanged from the wording issued a year earlier.

Meanwhile, the Supreme Court decision which effectively found that that it is impossible to monitor the threat of suicide, compared with other medical conditions, has implications which go beyond the issue of abortion. Indeed, it could affect future cases of medical negligence taken by the relatives of people who commit suicide and who allege lack of care on the part of a health care worker.

Dublin County coroner, Dr Bartley Sheehan, has been a long-time crusader for the decriminalisation of suicide and for a more sympathetic approach to the problem. Commenting at three inquests in 1991, he said that courts were not the best forum to hold such inquiries. He called on Irish legislators to provide a proper forum where full inquiries into such deaths could be held without the present "whitewash operations" that existed. Dr Sheehan added that although hundreds of families were affected by suicide each year, nothing was done to get at the root of the problem. These are words which come from a man who has seen much suffering among families over the years and they should not go unheeded. Dr Sheehan supports the concept of a social post mortem being held after a suicide, to trace the factors in society which lead people to take their own lives.

A number of prominent Irish doctors have been researching the issue of suicide and attempted suicide for many years. One of these is Cork consultant psychiatrist, Dr Michael Kelleher. During my research for this book, I put a number of key questions to him. Firstly, what do we now understand of the link between unemployment and suicide?

Dr Kelleher: "There is not a clear-cut relationship between unemployment and suicide. Many suicides of employable age are employed at the time of their death. It would appear that dissatisfaction with job, threat of loss of job or recent loss of job is more important than being without work for a long period. There are no constants here however. The stress of having no work may be more important if one lives in a neighbourhood of high employment or if one's friends are in the main, satisfactorily employed. For many of our young, it may be the lack of a sense of vocation or social purpose which is the discriminating factor rather than a lack of work itself. Much modern factory and office work is humdrum and seemingly devoid of immediate social significance."

What are the most common methods of suicide here?

Dr Kelleher: "The most common methods of suicide amongst Irish men are drowning and hanging. In particular, railway suicides may be of local importance. So also death by firearms is of local importance among military personnel. This is particularly so in the North of Ireland amongst the RUC.

"Among Irish women, drowning and self-poisoning are the two commonest methods. Poisoning with single dose tricyclic anti-depressants in Ireland is less than 4 per cent. It makes up 2 per cent of male suicides and 7 per cent of female suicides.

"There is an increase in poisoning with paracetamol and also with poisoning from car exhaust fumes. Paracetamol should not be freely available without prescription and if it is, should only be sold in quantities which, if taken together, would not be fatal. Poisoning with car exhaust fumes could be reduced if catalytic converters were installed in all motor cars." Does he believe that the number of suicides here will continue to increase and if so, why?

Dr Kelleher: "Suicide rates in Ireland increased from 1970 to about 1982 and then appeared to level off until about 1987 when they increased again. The increase in male and female suicides however is different. Over the past ten years, there has been no significant increase in female suicides. Male suicides however since 1987 have been significantly increasing. The main increase is among the young and middle aged men.

"Reasons for the increase in suicide are neither clear or certain. There is evidence that the social fabric of society has changed with a fall in marriage rates, a rise in the number of children born out of wedlock, a rise in alcoholism and an increase in crime. All of these may suggest that social cohesiveness is altering and with it, the individual's own sense of belonging and social connectedness.

"Added to this, death by suicide is less taboo and references to suicide are now commonly made in the pop folk culture of the young. Religious attitude, practice and belief have changed."

In terms of intervention, what more can the health services/social services do to help prevent suicides?

Dr Kelleher: "The vast majority of people who take their lives are mentally ill when they do so. Many of these have depression and a significant proportion have either not been treated or received inadequate treatment in the month before their death. Clearly, there is a need for better recognition and more effective treatment of these disorders.

"After affected illness, alcohol and drug addiction are common associates of suicide. Any service which will reduce the prevalence of these disorders should have the effect of reducing rates of suicide."

What effect will the decriminalisation of suicide and attempted suicide have in terms of gathering statistics and attitudes in society?

Dr Kelleher: "The decriminalisation of suicide will have no great effect on gathering statistics on suicide. Now that suicide is decriminalised, the Coroner's Courts should be held in camera much as family law courts are, so that relatives have privacy in their grief. I have treated patients who first became depressed after details of their relatives suicides were published in the local press."

What effect, if any, does media coverage of suicides have in terms of gathering figures and attitudes in society?

Dr Kelleher: "Reporting trends on suicide is important because it focuses the attention of society on these matters. There is evidence, however, that reporting of suicides of popular figures in a manner that makes the event appear attractive, noble or admirable can lead to others following suit. This is particularly so amongst the young. There is adequate evidence for this statement from American, British and German research work.

"In Ireland, there are often local spates of copy-cat syndrome where each individual is known to another and undoubtedly the behaviour of one influences the behaviour of his companions. Overall however, it is probably of greater benefit to society that it faces the problems of suicide, parasuicide and self-poisoning in an open and scientific manner rather than turning a blind eye to the cost and devastation caused."

I asked Dr Kelleher if there was one important message he wished to give society about suicide?

SUICIDE IN IRELAND

Dr Kelleher: "Each suicide is a personal tragedy, affecting the life of an individual, his immediate relatives and friends as well as society as a whole. The contingent factors influencing the choice of suicide should always be examined.

"There is a need for an expert committee working closely with the CSO and the country's coroners to produce a brief, informed annual report on the trends in suicidal behaviour," he said.

The confidential Garda reports were introduced in Ireland by the CSO in 1967 to overcome the difficulty facing Irish coroners who were unable to record official verdicts of suicide. The exact criteria by which the Gardai decide whether a case was one of suicide is not known. It is understood however that the decision in these cases is based on the balance of probabilities.

When someone is found dead, the Gardai are immediately informed. If a death certificate is not forthcoming from a GP, the Gardai will inform the local coroner who then orders a post-mortem. If the post-mortem shows the death was due to natural causes, a death certificate is issued. If, however, as in the case of most suicides, the cause appears to be unnatural, then an inquest is ordered by the coroner. The Gardai will prepare the evidence following interviews with the relatives and friends of the deceased. The coroner's verdict sheet which is completed following the inquest will just record the medical cause of death. The verdict sheet and the case file is then sent to the Minister for Justice while separately, a death certificate is sent by the coroner to the Registrar of Deaths. The registrar later sends the details to the CSO for their statistical analysis. Because until recently, the coroner's death certificate could not list suicide, the confidential Garda form 104 for each case was examined by the CSO to see whether the investigating Garda believed the death to be due to suicide. When we hear or read in the media that a person has been found dead in unusual circumstances, but that the Gardai are not treating the death as suspicious, it may indicate a suicide has taken place.

The increase in official Irish suicide rates dates from around

1967. It was at this time also that the Code 'cause of death unde-termined' was introduced for the first time by the authorities to cover the many cases where suicide could not be decided with certainty.

Direct communication between the Central Statistics Office and coroners on suicides on a confidential basis has been recommended. Indeed, the need for improved contact with the CSO was highlighted recently after a CSO error in the number of official suicides in the Southern Health Board area for 1987 and 1988. Thirty-six suicides were accidentally omitted from the official CSO figures.

A change in legislation in Britain in 1962 allowed British coroners to censure or exonerate parties in an inquest but as yet Irish coroners have no similar powers. Irish coroners should be allowed to give their views more openly about a case of suicide. Some have been outspoken but by and large they are confined as to what they can say. We should know whether there was something more the social services could have done, action which could reduce further fatalities? These are the crucial elements in a case history we need to know.

A dual system of reporting death statistics to help obtain more accurate figures has been suggested. In Switzerland for example, the attending doctor fills out two certificates, one for burial purposes only - which avoids any mention of suicide - and a second confidential certificate which provides for the recording of suicide. This means that accurate suicide statistics can be gathered, while also preserving the confidentiality and privacy of the deceased's relatives and friends.

Consultant psychiatrist, Professor Tom Fahy of University College Hospital Galway believes it should not just be left to coroners to decide on suicide verdicts. He believes that despite the decriminalisation of suicide, coroner's will still be subjected to pressure to return open verdicts. "I support the idea of a dual reporting system. One death certificate would be issued for the burial and this would be a public one. A second certificate would include a list of possible causes of death, including suicide. This would be a private form used by the CSO." Prof Fahy believes that there is a gross discrepancy in the reporting of suicide figures, in some areas by as much as 40 per cent or more. Studies show that the official Irish suicide figures can be multiplied by a factor of between two and four, he says.

The Catholic clergy have expressed concern about the rising suicide rates in this country - but, in truth, have only recently become converts to the cause. In the past, the Catholic Church has been unwilling to allow the subject be raised in homilies because of "concerns for the feelings of parishioners who may still be grief-stricken from this kind of loss". The old Catechism did not mention suicide. However, in an unexpected development, the 1990 Lenten Pastoral was devoted to suicide, the first such pastoral by an Irish bishop. In his letter to the people of Ireland, *Suicide: A permanent solution to a temporary problem?*, Dr Dermot Clifford, Archbishop of Cashel & Emly, said that pressure on children at school and at home to achieve material success was one of the causes of the increasing suicide rate. He added that secular materialism was less adequate than traditional cultural values in providing the distressed with a reason for living. While the Pastoral letter was well-received generally, a number of priests expressed unease about reading it in the presence of people who had been bereaved by a suicide, especially in the recent past.

In 1993, Bishop Edward Daly of Derry also decided to address the issue of suicide in a pastoral letter. He expressed concern at the increased number of suicides which had taken place in his diocese. While the diocese had experienced a great deal of violence due to the Northern troubles, a considerable number of families had experienced intense grief of a different nature - due to a suicide. According to Dr Daly:

"The Church teaches that the deliberate taking of innocent human life is always wrong and sinful. The important word is 'deliberate'. The question must be asked about the state of mind of most people when they take· their own lives or attempt to do so.

Most authorities accept that the victims are in a state of helplessness prior to the act, a state precipitated by real or imagined circumstances which interfere with reasonable and rational thinking. In most, if not all cases, the victim is not in control of his or her actions when suicide takes place." Pointing to some of the possible causes of the increase in suicide, he highlighted unemployment, alcohol abuse, marriage breakdown and a weakening of religious beliefs.

"Enormous pressures, possibly excessive pressures, are put on children to succeed. There are the added pressures imposed by the ongoing political unrest and conflict in our midst. But these are only part of the explanation. Members of very good and stable families have taken their own lives in recent years for no apparent reason," Dr Daly said. Deep depression, mental anguish, heartbreak, a feeling of failure, hopelessness and despair, one or more of these or similar emotional upsets usually formed the prelude to attempted suicide, he added. To help prevent such tragedies, Dr Daly said a healthy and happy family life was enormously important. "A young person's best guarantee of coping with stress is a strong sense of his or her own worth."

Roman Catholicism is the stated religion of the vast majority of people in the Republic of Ireland. Death, Judgment Day, Heaven and Hell are major aspects of the Catholic doctrine. Recent years have seen a decline in traditional Catholic values reflected in a fall in church attendances and vocations to the priesthood. While reports show that in some areas, church attendance could be as low as 10%, a church report in 1991 showed that 82% of Catholics still attend mass regularly. Suicide is a mortal sin under Catholic church teaching if it is committed with a clear mind. If a person takes their own life with the full use of reason, full knowledge of the act and consent, then the church views this as a 'rational' suicide. It is gravely sinful because "no human being has a right to usurp God's authority". One cannot avoid the fact however fact that there were a number of prominent suicides in the Old and New testament and martyrdom is part of the christian tradition. The mental torture which plagued Irish families down the years when the burial of their loved ones on consecrated ground was refused by the Church because of suicide is a matter of some embarrassment these days.

Remarkably, it has been suggested that Pope John Paul 1 may have contributed to his own death, 33 days into the papacy, by failing to take vital medication. According to Robert Cornwell in his book, *A Thief in the Night*, there was evidence that the Pope ceased taking life-saving medication for a blood clotting condition "not through forgetfulness" but because "he could no longer continue as Pope." Cornwell believes that Pope John Paul 1 was tormented by the conviction that he was unfit for the papcy. While the Pope's niece, Pia Basso, has rejected theories about Cardinal Luciani being morally worn out, she has admitted that "in those 33 days he was too alone." According to Irish Archbishop, Dr Dermot Clifford, for those who commit suicide in a state of deep depression and whose minds were not functioning rationally - such circumstances would greatly lessen their moral culpability or indeed remove it entirely. In 1985, a Catholic priest in an Italian Alpine village committed suicide because of chronic loneliness. Fr Dom Trombetto had fallen in love with a local woman but was unable to fulfil his twenty-year desire. The 45 year old priest was ignored by his parishioners. Following his suicide, the church attempted to cover-up the death as being the result of a sudden illness. The story is compellingly told in David Rice's excellent book, *Shattered Vows*.

The consumption of alcohol has always held a special place in Irish society. Much of our leisure time in this country has traditionally been spent in public houses. Irish people have a penchant for celebrating; the smallest excuse will do. As a self-prescribed treatment for real psychological problems, alcohol is a thoroughly dangerous medicine. The impact of excessive drinking on marriages can be especially devastating. It results in great stress on partners. Some of the personal stories in this book identify an important link between suicide and alcoholism. An English study has shown that one third of all women admitted to hospital because of drug overdoses complained of their husbands drinking. In a special report by the Royal College of Psychiatrists in England, doctors warned that:

"The slow development of mental stress contributes to the appalling high rate of suicide associated with alcoholism - although this is also a section of the population at particular risk because of underlying psychological problems which may be present. Much greater awareness of the possible involvement of alcohol in suicide and attempted suicide is needed."

Many of us have at least fantasised about the prospect of killing ourselves or of being dead, at some time. Very often this is for no other reason than wanting to make someone else feel guilty for something they have done. Those who suffer from depression however may feel so low that they seriously consider killing themselves. It is like being in a tunnel with no light at the end. Manic depression is usually a recurrent illness with associated severe mood swings where people may have a strong tendency to commit suicide. According to Dr Greg Wilkinson, senior lecturer at the Institute of Psychiatry, London, around 15% of severely depressed people eventually commit suicide.

"Suicide is a major preventable cause of death and attempted suicide one of the most easily identified risk factors for future suicide. Half of those who commit or attempt suicide give some clue of their intention."

Other factors which, if spotted quickly, can help reduce the suicide rates are: reducing the toxicity of drugs and poisons; improving medical treatment for those who attempt suicide; better medical and personal recognition and treatment of mental illness and more access to medical and social services. Those on the front line of treating people at risk of committing suicide have identified some interesting features which highlight the differences between suicide and attempted suicide:

Suicide	Attempted-suicide
Fatal	Non-fatal
Premeditated	Impulsive
Rates increase with age	Rates decrease with age
Commoner in men	Commoner in young women
Drugs and violent methods	More drug overdoses

It is not uncommon for people with a serious illness, afraid of future pain, to speak of suicide. This often reflects a wish to avoid the pain and indignity of terminal decline. Some people will even have developed very detailed contingency plans for their suicide if their disease reaches a certain stage. Serious physical illnesses like cancer and senile dementia contribute to the suicidal risk, particularly if there is associated depression. AIDS patients are also a high risk category.

"Where sensitivity and discretion have not been provided, some people have felt sufficiently distressed to attempt suicide (a number have been tragically successful). Thoughts of suicide are common, normal and a temporary response to unavoidable life threatening news. People with HIV and AIDS want to live !"

(Dr. David Miller, *Living with AIDS & HIV*)

Health workers have found that suicide attempts can follow a patients' perception that their concerns about dying were dismissed or trivialised. The result can be an impulsive attempt aimed at showing that the patient really means business. When some patients are hospitalised, they will make it clear that they do not wish to be treated beyond a certain stage. Doctors will usually respect such wishes after a full discussion with the patient and medical colleagues.

"There is also the fortunate and increasing recognition of the difference between prolonging life and prolonging death. In the past a number of patients have said that their plans for self-destruction were formulated because they feared that hospital staff might not understand this vital distinction," (Dr David Miller).

Irish guidelines in the area of withdrawing life support revolve around a paper by Mr Justice Declan Costello published in the *Irish Jurist* in 1986. Although the issue has yet to be legally tested in the Irish courts, Mr Justice Costello has suggested that a doctor who takes a *bona fide* decision to end mechanical or nutritional support for a terminally ill patient is unlikely to face criminal prosecution. He advises that where an unconscious terminally ill patient is involved, the doctor may have a responsibility, after consultation with the patient's family, to discontinue life support. It is argued that the Irish Courts would likely make a distinction - as has been made in the American Courts - between a reasoned choice of a competent terminally ill patient that medical treatment end and, deliberate moves to end life. There has been virtually no public debate about this issue in Ireland. It touches closely on the issue of euthanasia referred to in chapter one. The British Institute of Medical Ethics, which has examined the issue of prolonging life and assisting death, has listed certain treatments which are acceptable to withdraw, among them, artificial feeding and antibiotics.

Under Article 12 of the Principles of Medical Ethics in Europe, a doctor may restrict treatment in the case of incurable terminal illness to alleviate further physical and emotional suffering. Ultimately, it is a decision for doctors, in individual cases, based on clinical circumstances and professional ethics. This is a legal minefield which needs urgent clarification. Irish AIDS patient, John Mordaunt attempted suicide twice after he was told in 1986 that he was HIV positive. Up to then, he had been a hero-in addict for nearly half of his life. He recounted the period when he reached his lowest ebb in John Masterson's moving biography of his life:

"I was lying at home and I began thinking about the situation I was in. I began to ask myself why was I continuing on with this struggle. So I went downstairs and got a cup of tea, said goodnight to everybody and went upstairs and took every tablet I had. I got into bed and pulled the covers over my head. That's all I remember. And for some unknown reason my sister decided to come up and check on me and she found me just beginning to go completely out of it."

John was rushed to St Vincent's Hospital in Dublin and spent four days recovering there. Describing his suicide note "Goodbye Ma and Da. Sorry for all I put you through. Tell the lads I love them," he says that it started with the best handwriting writing and became progressively worse.

"I remember when I woke up just thinking. Oh no, I'm still alive. I couldn't believe it. I felt absolutely desperate, depressed, hopeless, helpless and useless."

Today, he works for Frontliners and the Terence Higgins Trust and is a AIDS counsellor and lecturer.

The risk of a suicide attempt is greatest when the person is emerging from a severe depression, according to Dr Patrick McKeon, consultant psychiatrist at St. Patrick's Hospital in Dublin:

"It is as if they lack the initiative and planning ability during the more severe phase of the illness. When your best efforts to cheer a depressed person up and attempts to show them the positive side of their lot are thwarted, it is likely they have reached the ultimate in despair."

While a person who is so intensely depressed may not actively be considering suicide, the degree of despondency he experiences will almost inevitably mean that it has crossed his mind, Dr McKeon warns.

It is not always easy to tell when a person is suicidal. Those who are determined to end their life will usually find some way of doing it, despite obstacles. As doctors are one of the main sources of powerful drugs, it is inevitable that those who commit suicide with drugs will probably have obtained them from their GP. While the profession argues that this does not necessarily make doctors in any way negligent, they remain key players in the suicide scenario. A study in the British Medical Journal in 1975 found that two-thirds of suicides visited their GP in the month prior to the suicide and that 80% of people who attempt suicide use drugs prescribed by doctors. In America, a study in the Journal of the American Medical Association found that doctors under forty were at least four times as likely as others to commit suicide.

The investigation of suicide introduces us to another key area that of the forensic scientist.

"If murder by poison is the forensic toxicologists caviare, his bread and butter form at least 99% of work from five other sources ... suicide; accidental poisonings; alleged attempts to poison food and drinks; malicious poisoning of animals; racehorse and greyhound doping."

(Dr H J. Walls, former director of the New Scotland Yard
police laboratory)

Dr Walls recounts that in his thirty years experience of forensic medicine, there is almost no poison which the determined suicide will not take. Over the years, suicides from town gas declined with the introduction of non-poisonous natural gas. As a result suicides from aspirin and barbiturate overdoses increased. One fascinating case is recounted.

A farmers wife was found shot with her body slumped over the end piece of an agricultural machine. A discharged shotgun lay beside her with the muzzle pointing at and almost touching her head with its butt wedged against part of the machine. The cause of death was obvious. Half of her head was missing and her brain was scattered over grass and bushes some twenty-five feet away. The question was - had she done it herself - it looked like a case of suicide?

The shotgun is an awkward weapon and the would-be suicide usually has to push the trigger at arms length. Work at the New Scotland Yard laboratory established that in the hard wood of the butt, there was quite a deep dent, bearing crushed-on paint identical with that of the machinery. The woman had obviously made use of the machinery to hold the gun in position while she fired it; the recoil had driven the butt hard against a projecting bolt-head. Her glasses were found in a position in which she must have laid them down carefully before shooting herself. Following a post-mortem, nothing else was discovered.

The most immediate difference an experienced forensic scientist encounters between a murder or suicide and a natural death is rarely horror or revulsion, but rather incongruity. "The body looks so patently out of place in normal everyday surroundings. It is, says Dr Walls, "an affront to the established order of things."

The treatment of Jehovah's Witnesses who on religious grounds refuse life-saving blood transfusions raises major ethical questions for doctors. These patients are at great risk of killing themselves. Should a doctor abide by the patient's wishes and teachings of their faith and allow them to die; or should he intervene and do everything in his power to save the person ? Some would argue that in refusing to have a transfusion, Jehovah's Witnesses in effect are committing suicide. Legal advice directs that if a patient refuses blood or blood products and the doctor proceeds and administers, he may end up in court on a charge of assault. In 1990, a Canadian doctor was ordered by the Supreme Court of Ontario to pay a patient $20,000 after he gave her a life-saving blood transfusion. Most of Jehovah's Witnesses now carry a card which reads...

"No Blood Transfusion! As one of Jehovah's Witnesses with firm religious convictions, I request that no blood or other blood products be administered to me under any circumstances. I fully realise the implications of this position but I have resolutely decided to obey the Bible command 'Keep abstaining from blood.'"

In the case of the Canadian Jehovah's Witness, the card added that the Witness had no religious objection to the use of non-blood alternatives. If a doctor is not in sympathy with a patient's wishes in refusing a transfusion, he can offer to refer the patient to someone else - if there is time. In any event, doctors must record in great detail all conversations with the Jehovah's Witness. In the case of infants, the approach is different. In good faith, a doctor can move to make a child a ward of court if he feels that life saving treatment is vital. In America, some parents of the Christian Scientists sect are being prosecuted by the State on charges similar to manslaughter for allowing their children to die from minor complaints without seeking medical attention. In Britain, some years ago, the social services department of an English county council applied to have a child of a Jehovah's Witness, who was under eighteen years of age, made a ward of court, in order that a life-saving blood transfusion could be administered.

For the Jehovah's Witness, a blood transfusion goes as fundamentally against their religion as for example a compulsory abortion might be against the wishes of a Catholic, even if the life of the mother was threatened. These are some of the life and death issues professionals on the front line face, on a daily basis.

CHAPTER FIVE

IN THE SPOTLIGHT

Barely a week goes by without news of a suicide or attempted suicide by a famous personality. Could it be that deaths by suicide are becoming less of a shock to us all - more accepted as a reality of the pressures of contemporary life? Links have been made between media coverage of suicide and increased youth suicide rates. It has also been suggested that the very talk and publicity about suicide prompts some people to kill themselves or attempt suicide. In the aftermath of suicide publicity, deaths by suicide have been found to increase. Rates have been found to be highest in areas closest to the reported suicide incident and in districts where media coverage of the event was greatest. Copycat suicides pose disturbing questions about the nature of media coverage in the wake of these events. The media has an enormous responsibility in this area. Following a dramatisation of suicide through drug overdose in the British television programme, *Eastenders*, an increase in attempted suicides was recorded in the London area. The portrayal of an attempted overdose using aspirin and alcohol in *Coronation Street* on New Year's Eve in 1990 also came in for some criticism, especially given the emotions connected with this time of year. Suicide is an issue which can attract great media attention. In America, where freedom of expression is a preciously-guarded right, a virtual do-it-yourself guide to suicide, became a bestseller in 1991. The book, *Final Exit,* provoked widespread criticism and there were widespread calls for it to be banned, even in this country.

The notoriety attached to both the known and suspected suicides of some well-known personalities has perhaps caused us to be less shocked at news of a death by suicide. Many famous names have hit the headlines in recent times, with questions surrounding the circumstances of their death. Speculation still surrounds the mysterious death of tycoon, Robert Maxwell found in the sea off the Canaries following a cruise in his yacht. The publishers' empire was facing major financial problems at the time. On the other hand insurance companies are liable to pay out around £20 million if Mr Maxwell died from natural causes. However, the evidence suggests suicide is more compelling than any other cause.

The death by suicide in 1993 of the defeated French prime minister, Mr Pierre Beregovoy shocked his country. He had been one of the most respected figures in the Socialist Party and always appeared to be a man of calm character. He shot himself in the head with his bodyguard's pistol and died while being transferred to a hospital in Paris. In the lead up to the suicide, Mr Beregovoy faced a difficult election campaign. His record in office as prime minister had come in for severe criticism, particularly due to the mounting public deficit and allegations of corruption which hurt deeply. His reputation had been built upon honesty and integrity and in the weeks prior to taking his own life, friends say he was very depressed.

One of the most tragic cases of recent times was the death of bride to be, Julie Statham from Dungannon. She died from a suspected drugs overdose at home just one month after UVF gunmen murdered her fiance and his father. An only child, friends said she died from a 'broken heart.' While the post-mortem results showed she died from a drugs overdose, it is possible that her action may not have been intentional. Just hours before her death, she applied to attend seminars at Queens University, where she was a final year student. Her ambition was to teach politics. Following the death of her boyfriend, she placed a death notice in the *Irish News* which read:

"In the darkness you are my clair de lune,
In the noise you are my peace and calm.

SUICIDE IN IRELAND

In troubled times you are my greatest comfort.
When I hold you all seems right with the world,
and I love you forever no matter what."

Suicide is no respecter of social class: those who take their
lives come from every level of society. Remember, the suicide of
comedian Tony Hancock, probably the most popular comedian in
Britain during the 50s and 60s. His body was found in a Sydney
Hotel room in 1968. Some time previous, he had also committed
'professional suicide' by attempting to dispense with the main
scriptwriters for his highly-successful show, Hancock's Half Hour.
The sixties also saw the tragic death of Beatles manager, Brian
Epstein, found in a London bedroom following an overdose of
sleeping pills. This was period which brought us the Profumo
Affair which revealed that the then Secretary for State, John
Profumo was found to be consorting with an alleged prostitute, a
fact he had expressly denied in the House of Commons. It was at
the flat of Dr Stephen Ward, an eminent osteopath that Profumo,
who was married, had consorted with this woman. Following the
scandal, Dr Ward was arrested for allegedly living off immoral
earnings. He committed suicide after the judge's summing up in
the case.

Questions still remain about the death of Rock 'n Roll King,
Elvis Presley in 1977 at his Mansion in Graceland, Memphis,
Tennessee. Presley's death was believed to have been due to drug
overdose but whether this was deliberate may never be known.
Prior to his death, however, the singer was addicted to tranquilliz-
ers and barbiturates.

There have been many other suspected suicides among media
stars : British actress Jill Bennett in 1990 and the outrageous Sex
Pistols punk group singer, Johnny Rotten. Guitarist Jimmy
Hendrix died in 1970 of a drug overdose and just one month later
blues singer, Janis Joplin died under similar circumstances.

One of the most highly-publicised suspected suicides of all
time must surely be that of actress Marilyn Monroe, found naked

in bed in her bungalow near Hollywood. An empty bottle of Nembutal sleeping tablets lay on her bedside table. Earlier that fateful day, she had telephoned her GP, Dr Ralph Greenson, about sleeping tablets. At 8pm in the evening, she went to bed saying "Goodnight honey" to her housekeeper. The rest is history.

The circumstances surrounding the death in 1981 of American actress, Natalie Wood also suggests a possible suicide. The star of such famous films as 'West Side Story" and 'Rebel without a Cause' was discovered floating face down in the Pacific, a short distance from her yacht. Some time before her death, Natalie had been arguing with her actor husband, Robert Wagner. The official police report said that she had slipped from the side of the boat. The pathologists report showed a high alcohol level. The attempted suicide of Loredana Berte, wife of the former tennis ace, Bjorn Borg received widespread publicity in the Spring of 1991. The 40 year old Italian pop singer had left a note "commending my soul to God." Following a tip from a friend of Loredana, Police broke into the singer's flat after hearing moans inside. In 1989, Bjorn Borg himself was rushed to hospital following an overdose of drugs, although he later rejected reports that it had been an attempted suicide.

Some suicides have made their special mark on world history. Austrian-born dictator Adolf Hitler, at the end of World War II, cornered in the ruins of Berlin by the Russians, made a suicide pact with his companion Eva Braun. He was later discovered on a sofa with gunshot wounds in his mouth. Eva Braun had taken poison. Following the collapse of the 1991 coup against Mikhail Gorbachev in Russia, one of its leaders Boris Pugo, the interior minister, committed suicide. He shot himself with a revolver in his Moscow flat just minutes before he was due to be arrested. His wife also shot herself.

Some literary greats have taken their own lives - Ernest Hemmingway, Sylvia Plath and Virginia Woolf, to name but a few. Suicide is encountered among every social class, every profession, among the greatest and weakest of men and women.

These cases represent the public face of suicide, the tip of the iceberg. We hear little of the private grief, the personal sorrow, guilt, anger and remorse experienced by families and friends of those who take their own lives. Unlike death from natural causes, or by accident, a death by suicide sends tremors of shock through our very souls. In order that we bring some meaning to the tragedy of suicide, and gain a better understanding of the underlying causes, we must begin to speak of the unspeakable. Suicide and attempted suicide are serious matters. Humour and suicide must seem like the most unlikely of bedfellows. Yet, supposedly as the animals with higher intelligence, we tend to find humour in some of the most unlikely subjects. Perhaps it makes accepting the truth that little bit easier. Suicide has occupied the minds of many writers and philosophers throughout history.

In Modern Manners (1983), P J. O'Rourke wrote of suicide:

"Guns are always the best method for a private suicide. They are more stylish looking than single-edged razor blades and natural gas has gotten so expensive. Drugs are too chancy. You might miscalculate the dosage and just have a good time."

German Author and philosopher, Friedrich Nietzsche offered a more unusual view of taking one's own life in Beyond Good & Evil, (1886):

"The thought of suicide is a great consolation: by means of it one gets successfully through many a bad night."

Suicide is understandably a very emotive subject and insensitive reference can cause deep distress. The unlikely topic was even the subject of a number one record in the 1970s with the theme music of the American television series MASH and its memorable chorus line "suicide is painless."

In 1990, the British heavy-metal rock band Judas Priest were taken to court in America for allegedly causing two of their fans to shoot themselves. It was claimed that one of their records contained subliminal messages to "Do It." Eighteen year-old Raymond Belknap held a sawn-off shotgun to his chin and died instantly from a single blast in December 1985. Another young man, James

Vance blew off the lower section of his face, but survived horribly mutilated for three years until his death in 1988. One of the songs by the band 'Beyond the Realms of Death' contains the following words:

"Yeah, I have left the world behind. I am safe now in my mind. I'm free to speak with my own mind. This is my life, this is my life, and I'll decide, not you."

The trial involving the band focussed on whether there was a second, virtually inaudible set of lyrics on the song whispered in the background as a subliminal message. Lawyers for the families argued that the two fans had formed a suicide pact after drinking beer, smoking marijuana and repeatedly listening to the *Stained Glass* album. The defence lawyers argued that it was the young men's troubled lives, including a history of drug and alcohol abuse, psychiatric disorders and physical abuse that had pushed them over the edge. The plaintiff's lost the case.

In another prominent suicide case, the top American chat show host, Oprah Winfrey, was sued following a claim by the family of Michael LaCalamita that his hour-long appearance on her show had shattered him and had caused him to end his own life.

"Oprah crucified my boy on national TV," his father said after Michael, aged 28, took part in a show about friends who are a bad influence. Two weeks later he was discovered hanging by a rope at his Illinois home. In the show Oprah told the audience that while Michael was married it did not prevent him from being a bad influence on his best friend, keeping him out late - drinking, dancing and a little flirting. His family claimed that the show portrayed their son as an insensitive person and that when he later saw a tape of the show it completely destroyed him. The case has yet to be decided.

Suicide comes in for plenty of mention down the years in literature, often in the form of black humour. Many writers have drawn inspiration from the subject, one always sure to stir deep emotions. Writer Cyril Connolly, taking a stab at the stigma of suicide in *The Unquiet Grave* (1944) wrote:

"There are many who dare not kill themselves for fear of what the neighbours will say."

Dorothy Parker brings the subject into verse in the cryptically titled Enough Rope 1926, and advises:

"Razors pain you;
Rivers are damp;
Acids stain you;
And drugs cause cramp.
Guns aren't lawful;
Nooses give;
Gas smells awful;
You might as well live."

To end this delve into the literary archives on the subject, perhaps the most touching and poignant of all literary references to suicide is by British poet, John Keats. His Ode to a Nightingale contains the most memorable line of all:

" I have been half in love with easeful death."

CHAPTER SIX

CLOSE TO THE EDGE

"Thank God I heard my children laughing and running through the hall. That snapped me out of it. The suicide impulse lasted only a moment - but that's all it takes."

- A well-known actor who, after placing the muzzle of a revolver into his mouth and feeling for the trigger, suddenly heard the voices which were to save his life.

According to Dublin-based consultant psychiatrist Professor Patricia Casey there are no accurate figures available on attempted suicide in Ireland since many people who indulge in 'self-harm' do not report it. Figures from Britain suggest that the rate is about 250 people for every hundred thousand of the population. On this basis, we could estimate the number of attempted suicides in Ireland each year to be over 8,700. What does Prof Casey see as the principle medical treatment for those at risk of suicide?

Prof Casey: "The treatment depends on the cause. Those who are at risk of suicide because of some crisis in their life, for example, a broken relationship may need very brief hospitalisation during this crisis period.

"During this time, they will be given support and advice as well as the opportunity to ventilate their feelings. Such patients in my experience respond within a few days once they have distanced themselves from the source of the crisis. Medication generally has no part to play in this group.

"Those who are at risk of suicide because of depressive illness or schizophrenia require treatment of those conditions with the appropriate drugs. Alcohol abusers who are at risk of suicide require detoxification and alcohol counselling subsequently. In all instances, those who are actively suicidal require in-patient treatment.

"It must be remembered however that the ability to predict suicide in the long term is extremely low. A number of studies demonstrate that because suicide is a very rare event, the ability to predict it, even in a high-risk group such as those who have recently attempted to harm themselves is extremely low. At best, suicide can only be predicted a few days into the future and it is for these the treatments outlined above are necessary. There are no biological markers to identify those at risk of suicide."

In her view, what are the most common methods of suicide in Ireland ?

Prof Casey: "Studies in the late 60s and early 70s in Britain and the US indicated that virtually all of those who committed suicide were suffering from serious psychiatric illness, particularly depressive illness and alcohol abuse. These studies have not been replicated. However, it would seem that psychiatric illness is forming a far less important part in causing suicide and the increase in rates is postulated to be associated with changes occurring in European society in general. In particular, the shift from traditional values, marital breakdown and economic recession, all being cited as contributing to the problem. The isolation which the individual may feel is also cited as a factor. These sociological theories are not new and were argued very cogently by Durkheim.

"Some people have speculated that unemployment *per se*, causes suicide. There is no evidence to suggest this, nor is there any evidence to suggest that poverty does. However, both in the context of other social factors and in the presence of ideological and social change, it may increase the risk," she said.

It has been suggested that people who attempt suicide may be unable to communicate their problems in a normal way. There are three distinct types of groups who attempt suicide. People who attempt to kill themselves through overdose are usually at low risk; those who repeatedly attempt suicide overdosing and cutting their wrists are at moderate risk, while people who use violent methods are at most risk.

Over 7,000 people are seen at Irish hospital casualty units every year with suspected poisoning. Those who are admitted alive have a better chance of survival now than ever before because of improvements in modern emergency treatment. Only a small number of adults and children, admitted alive with poisoning, actually die following treatment in intensive care. Some who never reach hospital alive because of self-inflicted poisoning are reflected in the official suicide statistics. There is little doubt that the majority of Irish adults - admitted to hospital for poisoning - have attempted suicide. In the case of children, it is usually a genuine accident.

The most common drugs in poison cases are the anti-depressants, sedatives and tranquillizers. Paracetamol and aspirin are also popular. Excessive alcohol is another. Many of the poisons deaths in Ireland are not due to drugs but household products like paint-thinners, turpentine and petroleum. These are much harder to treat in casualty than the more common poisons which doctors are more experienced in dealing with. While some doctors continue to use a tube to pump the stomach of a patient who has taken an overdose, many now prefer the administration of new drugs, which make the patient sick and cause the stomach to empty. There is a punitive aspect to stomach pumping with the tube. It should never be given without the patient's consent, unless the person is unconscious, as it can cause injury.

At the Poisons Information Centre in Dublin's Beaumont Hospital figures show that people who poison themselves with pre-scription drugs are usually young and their prospects after treatment are better. The most common drugs used are antidepressants. Those who use household or industrial products are usually older, remain longer in intensive care and are at high risk of death. Among the household products used are paint stripper, white spirits, corrosive cleaner, hammarite and even a rubber plant. As long as very dangerous compounds are commercially available, deliberate suicidal poisoning with these products will continue.

Establishing the extent of attempted suicide in Ireland poses major problems. This authors' figures are based on interviews with psychiatrists and research material. Attempted suicides in the domestic setting often go unrecorded. Those brought to the attention of a GP are not recorded for official purposes. Even when some patients are admitted to a hospital casualty unit with a suspected overdose, most will be discharged without being interviewed leaving us with no definite confirmation of a suicide attempt.

One of the country's leading casualty consultants has told this author that Dublin's main acute hospitals have to deal with around four attempted suicides a day. Dr Peter O' Connor, casualty consultant at the Mater Hospital in Dublin, says that many of the attempted suicides involve the widely available drug paracetamol. His estimates would put the number of attempted suicides seen at Dublin hospitals alone at nearly 1,500 a year. Unlike attempted suicides, most suicides leave a trail of unanswered questions. The trouble with attempted suicide is that people who attempt to kill themselves are at high risk of eventually succeeding.

To illustrate the difficulty facing coroners, consider the case of a man killed by a train some years ago. He had previously spent five years being treated for neurotic depression. At the inquest, the coroner noted that the engine driver said that he saw the man beside the tracks, and had applied his brakes. However, at the last moment, the man stepped in front of the engine rather than getting out of the way. The legal verdict was accidental death as it was believed that the man was trying to avoid the train, had become confused and jumped the wrong way. The psychiatric assessment was quasi-suicide - he had expressed suicidal feelings when he was being treated in hospital for depression and had previously taken an overdose. Doctors agreed that his mental state had contributed to his death.

A number of fatal road accidents in Ireland have also raised similar questions as to whether suicide was intended. In one such case, a commercial traveller who had been working most of his life as a driver, was discovered to have diabetes. He was told by his employers that he could no longer use the company truck because of his condition. During his last trip, his truck was involved in a head on collision with a wall. No obvious reason for the accident could be found. According to Garda sources, a number of car 'accidents' investigated each year defy explanation, other than possibly being suicide related.

This author has also spoken to a number of Irish country doctors who expressed concern about the large number of drownings in their area, which might reasonably be suspected as suicide.

Apart from the psychological effect on family members, a suicide or attempted suicide can also have shocking repercussions. Take the following case of a man whose addiction to alcohol led to serious debts, fraud and marital friction. His wife had several times threatened suicide and said that she would take her child with her. Knowing that his frauds were soon to be exposed, and being a little drunk, the husband went downstairs during the night and gassed himself with the kitchen cooker. Although the door was closed, a draught carried the gas upstairs and killed the sleeping child.

While the public perception is that suicide occurs mainly among middle aged, old and depressed people, suicide among young children is also a reality. We hear little of it in Ireland, yet unhappily is does exist. Other countries are coming to terms with this disturbing fact. In a widely reported incident in May 1991, two fourteen year old girls committed suicide by sitting on a railway track where a commuter train ran them both down. The two girls from Illinois, who were best friends and basketball teammates, left a note saying that they felt "stressed out". The father of one had died a short time previous. Both girls had sat on the tracks covering their ears as the train arrived and the engineer was unable to halt the vehicle as it rolled through the town, according to police reports.

Cases of suicide in Ireland involving people throwing themselves in front of a trains are rare enough. Again, much depends on access to the method of choice. According to the Gardai, this kind of suicide is virtually always successful. Few people could ever be expected to survive a clash with a rapidly moving train.

Weighing up the risks of a patient committing suicide is fraught with problems. In one case, a doctor became aware that one of his patients, an 83 year-old woman, was planning to commit suicide. A letter from the woman's stepdaughter said that she intended to take her own life. Although the doctor met the patient many times to discuss the matter, she made it clear that she had no intention of backing down from her proposed action. She even told the doctor the date she would take her own life and how - with an overdose of paracetamol.

The doctor rang the coroner's office for advice and asked whether a post mortem and an inquest would take place after a suicide. He believed that this might dissuade the woman from carrying out her plan. He also asked the coroner what the consequences would be for him, given that he was aware that a patient was planning to commit suicide. Although strongly pressed by the coroner for the name of the patient, the doctor refused to give it on grounds of patient confidentiality.

Some time later, a senior police officer rang the doctor, having been contacted by the coroner about the problem. Again asked the name of the patient, the doctor refused to disclose it. He was warned that it was a crime to aid and abet a suicide, punishable by 13 years' imprisonment - and that his duty of confidentiality did not entitle him to refuse to identify the patient.

The doctor contacted his medical insurers for advice and was told to maintain confidentiality. He also sought a second opinion from a psychiatrist to see if the patient was in need of treatment under the mental health legislation. The psychiatrist found that the woman was a meticulous, self-confident person who could no

longer accept her progressive physical deterioration. She had pre-
pared a long term plan to take her own life if ever she became disabled. All her financial affairs had been put in order and she could
not be dissuaded from her decision. Satisfied that there was no
evidence of depression or psychiatric disorder, the psychiatrist
said that there were no grounds for admitting the patient compul-
sorily to hospital.

In the days which followed, the doctor visited the patient regularly. She showed him a note she had written asking that should
her suicide attempt prove unsuccessful, no medical treatment was
to be administered. The note also said that the doctor had
attempted to dissuade her from taking her own life. On the fourth
day, the doctor arrived to find that the patient had taken an overdose of paracetamol, along with a note. She was unconscious,
vomiting and convulsing. The patient was taken to hospital and
although she regained consciousness briefly, she died two days
later. The doctor was visited by the police who warned him that he
would be interviewed under caution. However, no criminal charges
were subsequently pressed. At the inquest, the coroner said that
he did not think that "any crime had been committed by the GP
and that it would have been a breach of his professional duty to
disclose the patient's intentions to any third party." There was no
evidence that the doctor had provided any assistance - indeed, he
had tried to dissuade the patient. A verdict of suicide was recorded.

A recent case in America of doctor-aided suicide has drawn
considerable attention. The doctor, Timothy Quill from New York,
had written an article in a medical journal about his relationship
with an anonymous patient identified only as Diane. He said that
Diane had rejected treatment for her leukaemia and wanted him
to help her die when she was ready.

Dr Quill wrote that after many meetings with the patient, he
gave her a prescription for barbiturates, making sure that she
knew how many pills she needed to kill herself. When the case
was publicised, the District Attorney's office started an investiga-

tion but reached a legal standstill.

"We have not been able to determine the identity of the person he describes in his article," the DA said. "It's hard to have a prosecution without a body."

A person who is convicted of aiding a successful suicide in New York can expect a prison sentence of around 15 years. Dr Quill said in his article, that after Dianes' death, he contacted the medical examiner and reported that she had died of 'acute leukaemia.' The examiner tried in vain to track down anyone who remotely fit the criteria. When asked to provide the information needed by the DA, Dr Quill said that he would give this through his lawyers - but only if granted immunity from prosecution. He added that he was under no legal obligation to provide the information sought.

The incident raises a very hot issue indeed. Many doctors admit that physician-assisted suicide has been around for years, only the techniques have changed. In the 1930s and 1940s for example, many patients suffering from cancer or heart disease were given prescriptions for opium and belladonna rectal suppositories. On occasions, a patient who used these suppositories to get asleep would not wake in the morning due to overdose. To relieve the pain and insomnia, patients would increase the medication. Were the doctors assisting suicide - or were the patients merely trying to prolong the beneficial effect of the drugs?

Some people will go to whatever lengths are necessary to commit suicide. Take the case of a man who helped his cancer-stricken wife commit suicide. He flew with his wife to Detroit because he believed assisted suicide to be legal in Michigan. He fastened a plastic bag around his wife's neck after she took sleeping pills. The defence at the subsequent murder trial was that aiding a suicide, as an act of love, cannot be a crime.

CHAPTER SEVEN

A TIME TO ACT

There is but one truly serious philosophical problem and that is suicide. Judging whether life is or is not worth living amounts to answering the fundamental question of philosophy.

- Albert Camus

What can be done to reduce the number of suicides in Ireland? Firstly, we must acknowledge that a major problem exists and one which requires urgent attention. Each single suicide tends to generate a brief cycle of public attention, explanation, concern and promise of social reform. A more thoughtful and constant approach is needed. On an individual level, there is a tremendous responsibility on each of us to be watchful for those at risk. We have seen how both suicide and attempted suicide are often covert matters. What advice can be given to families who want to help loved ones who they fear may be at risk? The Samaritans have provided a valuable list of the risks of suicide, signs to watch out for and the actions which could help save lives.

These risks are:

* recent bereavement, or the break-up of a relationship including violence in the home

* a downward turn in health, employment or finances

* a painful or disabling illness, or dependency on drugs or alcohol

* suicide in the family or by a friend; for teenagers, suicide in the same age group

The signs can be:

* being withdrawn and finding it difficult to relate to others

* talking about suicide or death

* putting affairs in order or giving away valued possessions

* expressing feelings of failure or lack of self-esteem

* dwelling on problems that seem to have no solution

* having no supporting belief or philosophy in life

* attempting suicide or self-injury, however tentatively

What to do for those who appear at risk:

* show your concern and affection

* get them talking about their feelings

* talk and ask about the person who has died or gone away

* do not avoid awkward subjects: show you want to understand

* do not say 'I understand', but try to reflect their feelings, however dark or morbid

* do not try to 'cheer them up': the bright side you see may only make their darkness seem deeper

* if in doubt, say nothing; silence can mean more than words

* do not criticise or say what you would do, or what you believe

* ask about suicidal feelings: you cannot "give someone the idea" and often they will welcome the opportunity to talk about it

A greater emphasis in schools on human relationships and support for people, especially parents lacking in life skills would be very helpful. We should examine recent initiatives in America and elsewhere where over 100 high school educational programmes on suicide have been set up, reaching around 180,000 students. The programmes increase awareness of suicide; identify at risk people and help them to cope. Some of the programmes have not been without their problems. A number of students have ended up more troubled by the actual suicide education programme itself. Obviously any such programme for Ireland would need to be drawn up carefully. Before we embark on such programme, we must first accept the extent of the suicide and attempted suicide problem in Ireland.

Research work must also be funded and supported, especially work on serotonin levels in the brain, which may help us to identify those at risk at an early stage.

We need to identify the factors which are causing an increasing number of younger men to commit suicide. While attempted suicide is a serious problem, it is not as serious as suicide. In general, attempted suicides do not contain serious plans to end a life. The number of attempted suicides also appear to be levelling off after a peak during the 60s and 70s.

For health professionals, especially doctors, given that predicting which patients will end their lives by suicide is plagued by uncertainty, if they should err, let it be on the side of caution.

Mistakes in prediction are fatal and irreversible. Continuing medical education programmes for doctors and other health professionals must include information about the diagnosis and treatment of suicide as well as improved communication between doctors and their patients.

In general, people can help in a very practical way by keeping a watch for those most at risk. If someone appears to be at risk, then families have a duty to try and help.

It is estimated that around 1,000 people kill themselves every day around the world. Suicide is peculiar to humans: there is no evidence that what appears to be self-destructive behaviour in animals is associated with a wish to die. During the evolution of man, the ability not only to kill animals and fellow humans, but also himself was discovered. There can be little doubt but that suicidal acts will continue to be committed. Is it possible that some anti-suicidal drug will be developed in the future? Until such a time, more support and treatment for those at risk and those affected by a suicide is needed. Suicide prevention is no longer the preserve of sociologists and psychologists. It is now a matter of public concern, spearheaded by lay organisations like the Samaritans who have been providing psychological first aid since 1953.

A substantial number of Irish people are directly affected by suicide. It changes their perspective on life and tragically, places them at a higher risk of suicide also. For this reason, community and professional support is vital. Society must provide support for the many thousands affected by suicide, to help them carry the burden.

Suicide should not be viewed as scandal. We are still in the dark about some of the factors and influences which are contributing to the increasing number of Irish suicides. What cannot be in doubt is the need for a further change in both legislation and public perception towards suicide victims and their families.

A TIME TO ACT

We need:

* an official investigation into suicide and attempted suicide in Ireland on a national basis, to establish the true picture and real causes

* to set achievable targets to reduce suicide in Ireland

* a proper forum for inquests into suicide, including a change in the law to allow coroner's the discretion to hold 'suicide' inquests in private

* suicide prevention programmes and more support for the bereaved

* improved reporting procedures between coroners, the Gardai and the CSO, providing for more accurate national suicide statistics

* a more compassionate view of suicide by society

* improved medical and social care for those at risk, in particular, more bereavement counselling and support groups

* better education for doctors and the social services on the risk factors for suicide and attempted suicide

* improved controls on prescription and non-prescription drugs

* better risk prevention for prisoners

Overall, a more compassionate approach is needed toward those who - in time of despair or otherwise - commit the final act.
Let God be the judge of their actions, not us.

BIBLIOGRAPHY &
MAIN LITERARY SOURCES

Clinical directors' position paper on suicide, Michael J Kelleher, Irish Journal of Psychological Medicine, February 1993

The increase in the suicide rate in Ireland, Maura Daly, Michael Kelleher, Irish Medical Journal, August, 1987

Suicide in Cork and Ireland, Michael J Kelleher and Maura Daly, British Journal of Psychiatry, 1990

Suicide and Clinical Practice in Ireland, A special symposium on psychiatry, The Consultant.

Risk factors and precipitants for suicide, H R Cattell, Modern Medicine of Ireland, January 1991

Vital Statistics, Central Statistics Office, Yearly Summary 1990

The Incidence of Suicide, Southern Health Board, August 1989

Suicides by Prisoners, William Hurley, Medical Journal of Australia, August 1989 (pgs. 188-190)

Changes in the Irish Suicide Rate, Drs Michael Kelleher & Maura Daly, Cork, Edinburgh University Press, 1989

Penguin Dictionary of Modern Quotations.

The Coroners Act 1962, Government Publications Office, Dublin

Clinical Medicine, Kumar & Clarke, Bailliere Tindall, 1987

Medical Negligence, Lewis, Charles J, Frank Cass & Co, 1988

Recent Advances in Medicine, Dawson & Besser, Churchill Livingstone,1987

Eighth General Programme of Work, WHO, Geneva,1987

Activities of Irish Psychiatric Hospitals & Units, 1988-91, D Walsh & A O'Connor, Health Research Board, Dublin

Handbook of Differential Diagnosis, S Soreff & G McNeil, PSG Publishing, 1987

Suicide and the Irish: From Sin to Serotonin, Prof Tom Fahy, RTE Radio 1 lecture, 1990 and *Mental Health in Ireland,* edited by Colm Keane, RTE

Assessing the Epidemiology of suicide and parasuicide, British Medical Journal,1988 Prof R D Farmer, Dept Community Medicine, Charing Cross and Westminister Medical School, London

Effect of availability and acceptability of lethal instruments on suicide mortality, Prof R D T Farmer, Westminister Medical School, London, Scandinavian Medical Journal,1990

116

The suicidal patient: scope for preventative action, Dr Brian Barraclough, Senior Lecturer Psychiatry, University of Southampton, Modern Medicine of Ireland,1988

Nothing for It, Image magazine, Kathryn Holmquist, Irish Times health correspondent, 1990

Report of Special Committee of the Royal College of Psychiatrists on Alcohol and Alcoholism, Tavistock Publications, London, 1979

Depression - BMA family Doctor Guides, Dr Greg Wilkinson, 1989

Living with AIDS and HIV, Dr David Miller, MacMillan Press, London, 1987

John Mordaunt, with John Masterson, The O'Brien Press, Dublin, 1989

Depression, Dr Patrick McKeon, Sheldon Press, London, 1986

Expert Witness, Dr H J. Walls, John Long, London, 1972

Learning from Disaster, Michael Phelan, Vol. 301, p. 1401, British Medical Journal, 1990

Suicide Rate, Dr Peter Kirwan, Letter to The Irish Times, December 6, 1990

Dail Report, November 29, 1990, Government Publications Office

The assessment of the suicidal patient, Dr Maura Daly, Irish Doctor, 1990

The Medical Price of Failure on the Farm/ Suicide - a mortal sin or mental aberration, Dr Pat O' Shea, Irish Medical News, 1990

Can we prevent suicide?, David Lester, New York, AMS Press, 1989

Life's Preservative Against Self-Killing, John Sym, Routledge, London 1989

Youth Suicide: The Physician's Role in Suicide Prevention, Editorial by Susan J. Blumenthal, Journal of the American Medical Association, December 26, 1990

Suicide and attempted suicide, E Stengel, Pelican, Harmondsworth, 1964

History of the Study of Suicide, G Rosen, Psychological Medicine, 1971

The Doctor - Father Figure or Plumber, Prof James McCormick, Croom Helm, London, 1979

Neurosis in Suicide, Andrew Sims, Macmillan, London, 1983

Psychiatry Made Simple, M T Haslam, Heineman, London, 1982

Depression, Jack Dominian, Fontana, 1981

Adolescent Suicide Attempters, D Shaffer & M. Rojas, Journal of the American Medical Association, December 1990

African Homicide & Suicide, Paul Bohannan, Princeton University Press, 1960

Murder followed by Suicide, D J West, Heinemann, London, 1965

The Savage God - a study of suicide, A Alvarez, Weidenfeld-Nicholson, London, 1971

Discovering Suicide, J Maxwell Atkinson, Macmillan, 1978

The Suicide Syndrome, Richard Farmer & Stephen Hirsch, Croom Helm, London, 1979

Theory of Suicide, Maurice Farber, Funk & Wagnalls, New York, 1968

The many faces of suicide, Norman Faberon, McGraw Hill, New York, 1980

Suicide & attempted suicide, Erwin Stengel, Hamondsworth/ Penguin, 1964 & 1970

Suicide in Victorian & Edwardian England, Olive Anderson, Oxford, Clarendon, 1987

Life's preservative against self-killing, John Sym, Routledge, 1988

Lying, despair, jealousy, envy, sex, suicide, drugs and the good life, Leslie Farber, Basic Books, New York, 1976

Attempted suicide - a practical guide to its nature and management, Keith Hawton/Jose Catalan, Oxford University Press, 1982

Do Statistics lie ? Suicide in Kildare - and in Ireland, Dr Dermot Walsh et al, Psychological Medicine, 1990

Suicide rates in Ireland, M Clarke-Finnegan, T Fahy, Psychological Medicine, 1983

Suicide in Dublin, P McCarthy, D Walsh, British Medical Journal, 1966

The underreporting of suicide and the consequences for national statistics, British Journal of Psychiatry, 1975

A psychiatric approach to the diagnosis of suicide and its effects upon the Edinburgh statistics, British Journal of Psychiatry, 1973

The recent increase in reported suicide in Ireland, D Walsh, Journal of the Irish Medical Association, 1978

Unemployment, Poverty and Psychological Distress, C Whelan, D Hannan & S Creighton, ESRI Report, 1991

Suicide in a rural Irish population, P Kirwan, Irish Medical Journal, 1991

Suicide in Ireland, Drs M Clarke-Finnegan, T J Fahy, Psychological Medicine, 1983

Psychosocial characteristics of suicide victims in Dublin, Dr Sheila McGauran, Dr Michael Fitzgerald, Eastern Health Board, 1991

Suicide in Cork and Ireland, Drs Michael J kelleher, Maura Daly, British Journal of Psychiatry, 1990

Mental Health in Ireland, Colm Keane, editor, RTE/Gill and Macmillan,1991

Shattered Vows, David Rice, Blackstaff Press, 1991

The Samaritans, Dublin Report, 1992

Suicide, British Medical Journal, Volume 308, 1994

Euthanasia, Suicide and Assisted Suicide, M J Kelleher, Irish Medical Journal, 1993

The Samaritans, Dublin, 1992 Report

A general practice management plan for depression, Dr Patrick McKeon, Forum Magazine, 1994

Young Suicide, Eamonn Holmes, Irish Independent, June 1992

118

Lawful withdrawal of life support, Medical Defence Union journal, March 1993

A catchment area study of suicides in Waterford, 1990, Irish Journal of Psychological Medicine, Vol 9 No 2

Suicide rates in an Irish rural population, 1989/90, Dr Peter Kirwan

Suicide: A permanent solution to a temporary problem? Archbishop Rev Dermot clifford, 1990 Pastoral Letter

The family doctors role in the assessment of suicide risk, Irish Medical News, January 1994, Prof Patricia Casey

Grief of a different nature, Bishop Edward Daly, Pastoral Letter, 1993

Scan Magazine, local magazine, Shankill, Co Dublin

ADDITIONAL SOURCES

Personal and private correspondence
Irish Medical News
Irish Medical Times
Modern Medicine of Ireland
World Health Organisation
Irish Medical Organisation
Irish Hospital Consultants Association
Irish College of General Practitioners
The Irish Press
The Irish Times
The Irish Independent
Department of Health, Ireland
Central Statistics Office, Dublin
Office of Population Censuses & Surveys, London
Journal of the American Medical Association
The Samaritans
Southern Health Board
Friends of the Suicidally Bereaved, Cork
Dr Tim Collins, special adviser to the Minister for Health, Mr Brendan Howlin,TD

A special thanks to all those people who helped to make this book possible.